WILD SHORES OF AUSTRALIA
This first edition belongs to…

_____

WILD SHORES OF AUSTRALIA

By Ron Fisher
Photographed by Sam Abell and David Doubilet

Prepared by the Book Division
Published by the National Geographic Society, Washington, D.C.

WILD SHORES
OF AUSTRALIA

By Ron Fisher
Photographed by Sam Abell
and David Doubilet

Published by
The National Geographic Society
Reg Murphy, President
and Chief Executive Officer
Gilbert M. Grosvenor,
Chairman of the Board
Nina D. Hoffman, Senior Vice President

Prepared by The Book Division
William R. Gray,
Vice President and Director
Charles Kogod, Assistant Director
Barbara A. Payne, Editorial Director

Staff for this book
Toni Eugene, Text Editor
Jody Bolt Littlehales, Art Director
Victoria Cooper, Senior Researcher
Susan A. Franques, Researcher
Ron Fisher, Cynthia Russ Ramsay,
Picture Legend Writers
Carl Mehler, Map Editor
Thomas L. Gray, Map Research
Michelle H. Picard, Louis J. Spirito,
and GeoSystems Global Corporation,
Map Production

Richard S. Wain, Production Project Manager
Lewis R. Bassford, Production

Jennifer L. Burke, Illustrations Assistant
Dale-Marie Herring, Editorial Assistant
Kevin G. Craig, Peggy J. Purdy, Samuel J.
Taylor, Jr., Staff Assistants

Manufacturing and Quality Control
George V. White, Director
John T. Dunn, Associate Director
Vincent P. Ryan, Manager
Polly P. Tompkins, Executive Assistant

Elisabeth MacRae-Bobynskyj, Indexer

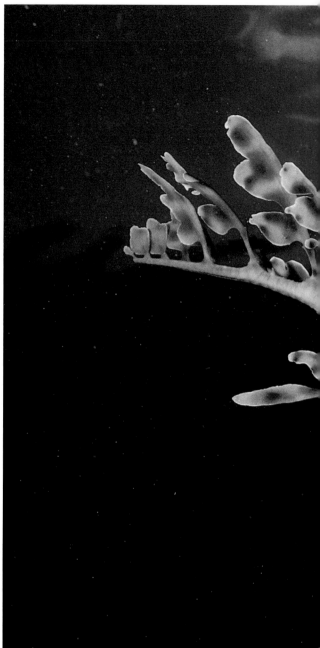

DAVID DOUBILET

Fish, not fantasy: A leafy sea dragon, its tattered appendages mimicking the seaweed of its habitat, swims through chill waters off South Australia. If the creature's camouflage does not deceive predators, it relies on its bony exterior for protection.

PAGE ONE: A species of kingfisher, the blue-winged kookaburra delivers a shrieking cackle reminiscent of manic laughter; two types of kookaburras inhabit Australia.
PRECEDING PAGES: Fury of a monsoon-brewed storm rolls over the Kimberley coast from the Timor Sea. During the wet season, downpours dump more than a foot of rain a month.

K*eeping faith with the past, Gordon and Alick Pablo, two elders from Injinoo,
an Aboriginal community near the tip of Cape York Peninsula, return
the skull of an ancestor to their homeland on Shelburne Bay.
Nearly 7,000 Aborigines live on the peninsula, a stronghold of native culture.*

FOREWORD

When people imagine Australia, they instinctively think of the outback—with sheep stations, the red center, and sunburnt plains. Yet it is the coastline to which most Australians relate. It is where most of them live, and it has a powerful influence on their thinking, their pursuits, and their attainments. It is no surprise that the nation excels at swimming, surfing, and yachting.

The coastline of Australia is very diverse, partly because of its extent and its geologic history, but also because it spans more than 30 degrees of latitude embracing great climatic changes. Traveling from the Great Barrier Reef, the world's largest area of coral, to the southern coastline abutting the great Southern Ocean, you are transported from a tropical environment of rain forests and turquoise blue waters to a realm where winter storms batter a rugged and often precipitous coast. The western shore above Geraldton is sparsely inhabited, offering huge stretches of stark coastline and an arid, forbidding hinterland. And yet it includes the world heritage area of Shark Bay, abounding in dugongs and dolphins. Much of the north and northwest coastline is protected by a maze of channels, mudflats, and mangroves. Sections such as Arnhem Land remain the province of the traditional owners, the Aboriginal people.

The appeal to many visitors and locals alike is the vast loneliness of much of the coastline. Even in the relatively well-developed and populated southeast corner of Australia you can walk beaches for miles without seeing another person. In the Great Australian Bight sheer limestone cliffs dominate much of the nearly 700 miles, guaranteeing a sense of wilderness where southern right whales from Antarctic waters gather to calve.

The coastline is now the scene of often bitter disputes between users, conservationists, and developers. On the eastern coast extensive and often ill-planned development has radically altered the coastline. There is an emerging realization that much of the coastal waters have been overfished. Many important fish species, including the barramundi, are decreasing in numbers.

Economically the coastline is of immense importance to the nation. Tourism is one of Australia's fastest-growing industries. Visitors are often lured by the continent's inland wonders. They come—from Europe, America, and Asia—and also visit such places as Sydney Harbour, the Queensland beaches, the Great Barrier Reef, and Victoria's "Shipwreck Coast." In fragile areas such as Kangaroo Island, visitor numbers are ballooning, and it will take careful planning to prevent the sites from being spoilt through overexploitation.

*C*linging to the coast of an arid continent, eight out of every ten Australians cluster in urban areas abutting the ocean. Only one-fifth of the land can support more than sparse settlement.

The coastline reveals much of the history of European settlement. Bays, capes, islands, and coastal mountains often bear English, Dutch, or French names given them by Cook, Tasman, and other navigators. These explorers were often precise observers and recorders of what they saw. The descriptions given by Matthew Flinders in the early 1800s still appear on some charts in use today. Almost every section of coast claims its share of shipwrecks, but the most prolific and tragic were those on the southwest coast of Victoria, where vessels frequently foundered in heavy seas as they sought entry to the safe haven of Port Phillip Bay.

With its vast, lonely stretches, its exposure to the violent elements of the oceans, and a recent history both harsh and romantic, Australia's coast can indeed be thought of as the "wild shores."

—John Landy, author of *A Coastal Diary: A Study of One of Australia's Wildest and Most Beautiful Coastlines*

Relics of an ancient forest protrude from sand dunes on Fraser Island. Immense sandblows that smothered these trees helped build Fraser, the world's largest sand island.

FOLLOWING PAGES: Largest and most dangerous of crocodiles, a saltwater croc seeks warmth on a sandbar near Cape York Peninsula's Shelburne Bay.

THE CORAL SEA

Photographed by Sam Abell

n the darkness, the ship's prow, like a blunt arrow, is aimed at a glittering coast. From atop the navigation deck at the rear of the ship, high above the water, a cold wind is in my face. The moon is scudding through tattered clouds behind me, and, before me, the lights of Sydney are a thin band of sparkle low on the horizon.

The *Columbus Victoria,* a German freighter three weeks out of Oakland, California, is still 15 miles from shore. For another hour we steam steadily ahead, the lights of Australia slowly growing nearer. A harbor pilot comes aboard, clambering up a Jacob's ladder in the darkness. The big ship slides slowly between the twin heads of Sydney Harbour, turns left, and creeps down an avenue of navigation buoys, their red and green lights deliberately blinking.

We turn right, and the Sydney Opera House, bathed in light, hoists its spinnaker sails upward into darkness. We are only yards away from it. We pass under the floodlit Harbour Bridge, our topmost antennae seemingly clearing it by just inches. At the very peak of the bridge's arch, twin flags snap in the breeze. We turn left again, barely moving now, and tugboats at our bow and stern nudge us around like a locomotive in a roundhouse and into a berth in Darling Harbour. Skyscrapers, many of their windows still ablaze in spite of the late hour, rise around us. We are docked in downtown Sydney, Australia.

Travel writer Jan Morris thought, "Few cities on earth can offer so operatic an approach."

A trip around Australia's coastal region is a ride on a splendid carousel. You can get off here and there—perhaps at a glittery surfer beach, or on a coast backed by endless miles of desolate bush, or at tropical rivers where the snouts of man-eating crocodiles break the muddy surface. Though much of the coastline is as wild as anywhere on earth, other stretches have been pretty well tamed. The wildest thing you're likely to encounter on the Gold Coast, for instance, is rampaging teenagers. It's wild in the same way that Fort Lauderdale is wild.

Australia has a coastline of some 22,800 miles. I didn't see it all in my clockwise tour, but I sampled as much as I could.

England's Capt. James Cook didn't see it all either, but it sometimes seems he did. Names he bestowed are everywhere on the east coast of the continent. He sailed past the bay where Sydney would grow and named it Port Jackson.

He was in these waters in 1770, after visiting Tahiti and circumnavigating New Zealand. He and his ship, *Endeavour,* were aiming for Tasmania—Van Diemen's Land, as it then was—but southerly gales drove them north to a new and unfamiliar shore:

today's Cape Everard in the state of Victoria. They sailed north along the coast, charting and observing and attempting to make contact with some timid Aborigines. "All they seem'd to want was for us to be gone," Cook wrote.

The trip up the east coast took Cook and his ship through 28 degrees of latitude, more than 2,000 miles. When the shore turned westward at the tip of Cape York, Cook landed on an island and hoisted the English colors, claiming the whole east coast of Australia in the name of the king. The coast he explored has been transformed in ways unimaginable to him. Queensland has been called the "California of Australia," though generally not by Australians, who might well think of California as the Queensland of North America.

Queensland has an enormous coastline all by itself, some 3,200 miles, though only about half of that, from Brisbane to Cairns, is easily accessible. Australians named Queensland the "Sunshine State," partly for its climate, but also for the magnificent beaches that stretch north from the New South Wales border. Those beaches and the Great Barrier Reef now attract crowds of tourists, who spend the equivalent of some six billion U.S. dollars a year. The southern Queensland coast is so heavily populated that people are getting in one another's way. Battles over development and growth are now common.

Disaster had nearly befallen Cook and his men on their trip up the coast. On the night of June 11, 1770, *Endeavour* struck hard and fast on a coral reef. The collision ripped a hole in the ship that nearly sank it. Unwittingly, Cook and his crew had run aground on one of the wonders of the natural world—Australia's Great Barrier Reef, a complex of islands, reefs, cays, deepwater channels, bays, and lagoons. It parallels the coast of Queensland and stretches some 1,250 miles from north to south. *Endeavour* was about 12 miles from land.

They got themselves off the reef, and, leaking badly, made their way up the coast, looking for a safe anchorage where they could repair the ship. They found the mouth of a river—which Cook named the Endeavour River—crossed its bar, and careened the ship alongside a steep beach on the south bank, the site of present-day Cooktown. Cook's crew spent seven weeks ashore here repairing the ship. Tents, a forge, a workshop, a butcher, and pens for pigs and sheep gave at least the appearance of a tiny village—and it was in fact the first known European settlement in Australia.

Cooktown's most conspicuous feature is Grassy Hill, an abrupt prominence that rises several hundred feet on the edge of town. From its breezy top—the same high grassy hill that Cook climbed—the prospect is much the same as he saw: sandbanks, shoals and the sinuous Endeavour River winding to the sea.

Most of the little town is visible from there as well. Today's population is 1,500; in the 1870s Cooktown held 5,000, with 37 hotels, 20 restaurants, and 32 general stores—all feeding a frenzied rush inland to the Palmer River, where gold had been discovered in 1873. Cooktown catered to 30,000 prospectors, but the boom didn't last, and as late as the 1930s the town still had no road connecting it with the rest of Australia.

There's a monument to Cook at the harbor, with an inscription: *Post Cineres Gloria Venit*—Glory Comes After the Ashes, a somewhat ironic statement of one so famous. I sat and watched the harbor activity for a while one brutally hot day. Anchored sailboats turned slowly in the breeze. The *Kangaroo Explorer*, a cruise boat that runs between Cairns and the tip of Cape York, was docked. Passengers were making their way through the heat to the ship for lunch. A matron all in white, beneath a flowery parasol, returned, kicking up a little puff of dust with each step.

In the fierce heat I made my way out to the edge of town to the cemetery. Tombstones of old cemeteries are always touching, especially those of children, and there are many here. One stone marks the graves of Matthew Ambrose Carroll and his six sons, aged between 25 years and six weeks. One section of the cemetery memorializes the many Chinese who died here. They came to work the goldfields, but the departed were shipped home to China; gold to pay for a funeral accompanied the remains. Frangipani trees were heavy with pink blooms, and a flock of gaudy parrots passed overhead, screaming like lost souls.

Today there are roads out of Cooktown to both north and south, but be prepared for a rough ride. Roads here turn into four-wheel-drive lanes that become bumpy, boggy tracks through the bush. Many people who want to see outback Australia put themselves in the hands of tour operators and outfitters who are equipped for rugged country. I explored south of Cooktown with Ken Lander of Billy Tea Bush Safaris. There were six of us— a Canadian, a British couple, an Australian couple, and myself. From Cairns we drove up the coast through lush farmland and the town of Mossman, where the region's plentiful sugarcane is processed, and took a short boat ride on the Daintree River.

Estuarine—or saltwater—crocodiles inhabit these waters in Australia's north. People argue about how big they get, but 18-foot specimens are not rare. Unlike their cousins, freshwater crocodiles, "salties" are dangerous and aggressive and will attack people unprovoked. Bill Smith, our boatman showed us a couple of little ones, one lying on the muddy bank, the other in shallow water, facing upstream, its mouth slightly open. "This year's model," Bill called them. He said, "The river's pretty shallow, but there are plenty of women on board to get out and push us off if we get stuck. Us blokes are not getting in that water. Those crocs are *man*-eaters." A sunbird nest—a long pendant with an entrance on the side made of bark, grass, leaves, and feathers and bound with cobwebs—dangled from a branch, as two tiny yellow-bellied sunbirds flitted around it. Great egrets stood scowling in the shallows.

Across the Daintree a primitive road took us up into the Alexandra Range for views of coast and rain forest. We lunched beside a stream and swam in its cool waters, with butterflies fluttering by and birds singing in the treetops. We touched the Coral Sea at Cape Tribulation, another spot named by poor Captain Cook that was inspired by his struggle up the coast.

Since it was November, swimming in the Coral Sea was out. Of all the things along Australia's coast that will eat you, bite you, or sting you, the box jellyfish is among the scariest. Box jellyfish are only about eight inches across, but their tentacles can reach nearly ten feet, and their sting can be fatal. In the summer beaches in north Queensland post warnings.

Cairns—pronounced "Cans" by Australians; I heard an American visitor murmur to his wife, on being welcomed by an airport bus driver to the city: "I can't hear an 'r' in there at all"—looks and feels like a tropical city, with its wide streets and palm trees and its mangrove-lined inlets. It hugs the coast south of Cooktown and is a gateway for visitors to the Cape York Peninsula as well as to the Great Barrier Reef, which is just offshore. The harbor's tidal edge, along the Esplanade, is a giant mudflat at low tide, filled with bad-tempered pelicans.

The Great Barrier Reef is the only living thing on earth that can be seen from the moon, several Australians proudly told me. It is a long ribbon of coral reefs and islands, teeming with a complex diversity of marine life: 400 species of coral, 4,000 species of mollusk, 1,500 species of fish. It is protected by Australia as the Great Barrier Reef Marine Park and recognized by UNESCO as a world heritage area.

In the 1800s phosphate companies mined guano from the reef's islands; in the 1920s soup canneries harvested green turtles. Despite its protected status a number of forces threaten the reef today. Increasing tourist traffic brings problems ranging from sewage disposal to reef damage from coral collectors and boat anchors. Deforestation and farming on the mainland send fertilizers and other pollutants running down rivers and into the reef's waters. The reef is healthy now, and its managers are working to reduce the effects of such threats and keep it that way.

Fifteen years ago there were very few offshore resorts on or near the reef; today they're sprinkled up and down its length. At them, visitors engage in everything from aerobics to windsurfing, with billiards, lawn bowling, and squash in between.

On Green Island, a 32-acre coral cay just 45 minutes by high-speed catamaran from Cairns, I was greatly outnumbered by Japanese tourists. By midmorning it was uncomfortably hot on the island, so I sat beside the pool and watched skinny legs turn pink in the sun. A lovely white sand beach was crowded with swimmers and snorkelers. At Green Island guests can do as much or as little as they wish. As a day-tripper, my afternoon was carefully scheduled: 1:30 p.m., semisubmersible; 2:00 p.m., glass-bottom boat; 2:45 p.m., rain forest walk. The semisubmersible was a small boat with a basement; the walls were of thick glass. We sat in narrow rows of two, peering out at the undersea panorama at our elbows. In the swell, the boat rocked alarmingly. It was like being in the gondola of a hot-air balloon, swaying in the breeze. The naturalist, a young woman from Scotland, spoke to us of the corals' "eggs and spairm."

Farther down the coast, I spent several days on Dunk Island, named by Cook for George Montagu Dunk, First Lord of the Admiralty. During World War II a Royal Australian Air Force radar station was built on the island, and the battle of the Coral Sea was controlled from here. I arrived by Quick-Cat from Cairns—"We call it the slow dog," a cynical waiter told me. The boat took us to Beaver Cay for a day on the reef.

I confess I'm not an enthusiastic snorkeler. I don't like the way the rubber mask clings to my face, like one of those creatures from the *Alien* movies. I don't like hearing myself breathe. I don't like the eerie way the light plays across the bottom, creating watery shadows. I don't like the way the depth of the water can change suddenly and alarmingly; it's like sticking your head out over the edge of a building. But I'll admit, if you enjoy snorkeling, this is the place for it.

Two British women were arguing about which was best, the semisubmersible or the glass-bottom boat. "You see more fish snorkeling," someone else said. It's true, you do. There are blue fish, green fish, and yellow fish; striped fish, spotted fish, and banded fish. It's like flying over an alien world: strange constructions, colors, creatures. Sea cucumbers, or bêche-de-mer, lie sluglike on the bottom. Fusiliers with yellow tails come and go. Red emperors, very common, have fetching zebra-like stripes.

Sergeant-major fish seem to demand a salute. An acre of reef may contain 200 species of fish.

On board the anchored QuickCat, a tape is playing "Nobody Loves You When You're Down and Out." In the distance, snorkelers in gaudy purples and pinks spout like whales when they surface. Passengers in the glass-bottom boat are all seated, leaning forward, peering through the floor. It looks like they're all being sick.

Just to the west of Dunk, on the mainland in Mission Beach, I happened onto a group fighting to save one of Australia's unique animals—the cassowary. Two species of large flightless birds remain in Australia: One is the emu, which can reach five feet in height and is common in rural areas all over the country. In the early 1990s, during a drought, emus began migrating in search of food, and herds of 600 occasionally were encountered, wandering along fence lines. It must have been a sight. The other large flightless bird is the cassowary, which is having a hard time of it. Shy and easily disturbed by development, it has had its range reduced to a thin strip of rain forest along the north Queensland coast.

The group in Mission Beach call themselves C^4—the Community for Coastal and Cassowary Conservation Inc. It is working to help save the cassowaries in the area. Driving through thick and spooky forest into Mission Beach, you're alerted to something different by yellow roadside signs—much like the familiar deer-crossing signs in the U.S.—warning drivers to be on the lookout for cassowaries.

"We have one or two birds killed on the road every year," said Mary Ritchie, vice president of C^4. We were having coffee and cookies in the group's headquarters on the edge of town. "Usually it's not tourists but locals who hit them. Tourists see the signs and slow down. Locals get careless."

C^4 had been recommended to me as a group of spirit and determination. "We meet socially as well," said Mary. "We enjoy good food and good company. We can't decide whether we're conservationists with a gastronomic flair, or gastronomes with a conservationist flair. Our priorities seem to be good food, good wine, and conservation." Nonetheless, the group has done a lot to help the endangered cassowary. The members hold "plantouts" during which they plant seedlings of native fruit trees, which the birds depend on for the fallen fruit they eat. They have planted more than two thousand trees already, and are encouraging local farmers to do the same. "Our basic source of seeds is cassowary droppings, because the seeds seem to germinate quicker if they've been through a bird." Members of the group are urged to carry pooper-scoopers on their walks to retrieve droppings. Droppings may be too delicate a word for what the birds leave behind. "They're *big* birds," laughed Mary. "They drop great big sloppy cowflops that look like piles of fruit salad."

Mary estimates that there are between 180 and 200 cassowaries in the 135 square miles of the conservation area. Nearly 10 percent of the human population of Mission Beach belongs to their organization, but not everyone approves. A somewhat mysterious fire destroyed their former headquarters on New Year's Eve in 1994. It may have been an accident, it may have been a prank that got out of hand, or it may have been deliberately set by someone opposed to the group's activities. "This time we're building with cement blocks," Mary said.

"We lost everything, including records that went back to 1989, all our clippings, files. It was sad, but still, no lives were lost, just material things. We're all still here."

Just down the coast from Mission Beach, near the little town of Cardwell, another environmental battle is being fought. I walked out onto the jetty of the little town and talked for a bit with two fishermen. They were from Sydney and spend a month each year traveling around together fishing. One said, "We travel together until our arguments—our 'debates,' my mate calls 'em—turn serious. Then we know it's time to go back to Sydney." Two dugongs surfaced briefly nearby. I said I understood there was a big resort planned for nearby. "On that point," said the other. "They're having a hell of a fight about it."

Margaret Thorsborne, a tiny, grandmotherly 69, with white hair and sparkling eyes, is one of the chief fighters. She welcomed me to her home at the end of a narrow driveway inside Edmund Kennedy National Park, named for an early explorer. There were wallabies on the grass, a tiny, darting skink under my chair, orioles calling, and honeyeaters at the open window.

Margaret and her friends went into action in 1994, when a developer made plans to build a resort on Hinchinbrook Channel, which separates the mainland from Hinchinbrook Island National Park. Novelist Nevil Shute wrote that the channel "must be one of the most beautiful coastlines in the world." Rugged, wooded mountains rise into the clouds just across the shallow channel from Cardwell. The developer—the same one my Fielding guide to Australia calls "infamous" for the heavy-handed way he built a resort on Hamilton Island—had acquired a big tract of land nearby. His plans call for a resort that will house 1,500 guests, with a staff of a thousand. Cardwell's population, by contrast, is only about 1,300, so the town would be dwarfed by the resort.

"For such a development to come here," Margaret said, "is like a nightmare."

The fight nearly came to blows. The developer persuaded the Queensland state government to grant him a permit to clear mangroves, even though they were in a state marine park. "So we went in," said Margaret.

"You mean you went physically in?" I asked.

"We went physically in. The mangroves couldn't be cleared if members of the public were present. We had a camp at each end of the site, and we were there every day for three weeks, from dawn to dark. Then another permit was granted, enabling the removal of the mangrove defenders. The heavy machinery came in." Margaret showed me photos of herself, standing with arms folded and a grim smile on her face, with the treads and buckets of earthmoving equipment missing her by inches. "We got up into the trees, and they would clear all around us, leaving just that one tree with a person in it." The chairman of the shire council had previously denounced such clearing as "mass murder of mangroves." The heat and the mosquitoes were fierce.

Police came and removed the protesters, but the next day they were back in greater numbers. Police took them out again. "There was a nice, friendly policeman; he removed me quite a few times." She showed me a photo from a newspaper of herself being escorted off the site by the giant policeman.

"That evening," Margaret said, "because of the threat the clearing posed to the adjacent world-heritage-listed Hinchinbrook Channel, the Governor General of Australia issued a proclamation to prevent further destruction. Late that night, however, floodlights went up, and the work and protests continued into the early hours. A few days later some local people with axes and chain saws destroyed more of the little that was left."

Despite the distress and destruction, Margaret can still smile at some recollections. "One day I was in another town and bought myself some flowers. In one of the shops a woman said, 'Well, you can't be as bad as people say if someone gave you flowers.'"

We drove to Oyster Point, where the battle took place, and walked along the muddy shore among dead, bulldozed mangroves, heaped like jackstraws. Margaret held onto her hat in the wind and looked up at me. "It was awful, just awful," she said. She and her friends are replanting mangroves, tiny green sprouts that look piteous against the black mud. Torres Strait pigeons flew over, flashes of black and white; they nest on the islands and feed in the rain forests of the mainland.

One of the saddest sights of the whole sorry affair, Margaret told me, was when a beach stone-curlew tried to chase a swamp dozer away as the dozer graded the beach crest. It ran frantically across the beach at the dozer with wings and neck outstretched, in a brave but vain attempt to protect its home.

"We need to leave some places unspoiled," Margaret said. "Must we take them all? We are not the last generation on earth. Will people of the future thank us for protecting this beautiful region, or will they say, 'How could you let this happen? How could you turn your back on the opportunity to save it?'"

Fraser Island, farther down the coast, is the largest sand island in the world—some 76 miles long by 3 to 15 miles wide. More than 230 species of birds inhabit it, from the Australian pelican to the yellow-tailed black cockatoo. There are echidnas and wallabies in the forests, and the Fraser Island dingoes—or wild dogs—are thought to be the purest strain remaining in eastern Australia. Distinctive satinay trees grow in the center of the island, and blackbutts line the tops of ridges. Scribbly gums have characteristic scribbles in their white bark, left by burrowing insects. Cypress forests edge parts of the mainland side of the island, and paperbark has adapted to the sandy environment.

Logging on Fraser was halted in 1991, and now it is mostly national park and vacant crown land and is a UNESCO world heritage site.

A comfortable resort—Kingfisher Bay Resort & Village—on the island's west coast prides itself on being ecologically correct. Major trees were spared during construction, and all buildings are below treetop level. Exterior colors and finishes blend with the surrounding bush. Native species from the actual site were used in landscaping, and a nursery was constructed on-site to care for the 150,000 plants required for the project. All solid waste is transported off the island, and natural convection currents cool the hotel complex instead of air-conditioning, saving some 500,000 kilowatt-hours of energy each year.

The resort has its own staff of rangers to help people enjoy the island. One of them, Dave Laycock, told me, "Fraser Island is a sand sculpture created by the wind." Giant sandblows along the east coast, powered by the winds, are gradually moving back through the forests and inland across the island. We climbed up onto one and watched the changing light etch shadows on its smooth face. At Lake McKenzie, one of Fraser's famous perched lakes—they sit on impermeable sandrock in depressions between sand dunes well above the level of the water table—tourists were swimming in the cool water. A butcher-bird sang a long, lovely song that sounded improvised. When Dave mimicked it, it started over from the beginning, again and again. "It can't stop," said Dave. At Central Station, a campground that was once a forestry station, dingo puppies played in the underbrush. One was chewing on somebody's baseball cap.

Another ranger, Scott Toohey, took me for a rain forest walk along Dundonga Creek. It was dark and cool deep in the forest. "Do you mind getting those shoes wet?" Scott asked, as he led me into the creek. It ran around our ankles without a murmur. "It's rocks that make a stream noisy," Scott said. "Here there are no rocks. Only sand." The silence in the forest was total.

"If you look at Fraser Island from the air, you'll see that it's a series of parallel sand dunes, all pushed from the southeast to the northwest by the wind. Each is a different age. The one we're on now is about 125,000 years old. The island is the world's greatest sponge. If it stopped raining today, there'd be enough water in the water table here to keep the streams on the island running for another 50 to 60 years." Treetops and bushes were busy with birds—honeyeaters and rainbow bee-eaters, shrike-thrushes and mistletoebirds and kookaburras.

Humpback whales were migrating south toward their summer feeding grounds off Antarctica. They often stop in Platypus Bay at the north end of Fraser Island for a few days en route, and I went out one day with a whale-watching boat from the resort to see them. As the big boat plied back and forth across the bay looking for whales, a baby cried and oldsters leaned their heads against pillars to nap. Tea and cookies were served. Four American women were having a good time. One told a joke whose punch line was, "The no-smoking sign has turned the captain on."

When whales were spotted, people rushed from one side of the boat to the other, scrambling for the best view. There were two whales, a mother and her calf. The captain turned off the boat's engine. We watched the two-month-old youngster breaching. It would leap into the air, turn onto its side, and splash down into the water. People stood on chairs and climbed the ladder to the roof for better views. Cameras chattered like cicadas.

The mother swam alongside the calf, breathing heavily and noisily, occasionally rolling over onto her side and waving a flipper in the air. Sometimes the youngster made a graceful leap and a solid *splash!* Sometimes it executed an awkward belly flop. Sometimes it threw most of its body out of the water, other times not much more than its head.

As the whales disappeared into the blue distance, the calf leaped into the dazzling air. And leaped again. And again.

*C*oiled around a small tree, a green python establishes a lookout in Iron
Range National Park, a swath of rain forest on Cape York Peninsula. During the day,
the snake usually retreats to a tree hollow or hides among leaves, where its color blends
with the foliage. Like the green python, other rare animal species inhabit
the Iron Range area and occur in New Guinea—proof that a land bridge
once linked Australia and the island. Sinuous buttresses (opposite) form the base
of a lofty fig tree in the park. Covering nearly 135 square miles, it preserves
the largest lowland rain forest region in Australia.

F*looding on the tip of Cape York Peninsula during the wet season causes calamities. "Four tow cables snapped before we could pull the front truck out of the mud," says photographer Sam Abell. Tranquil Cooktown, on the peninsula's east coast, earned a reputation in the 1870s, during the Palmer River gold rush, as a wide-open community where 30,000 boomers caroused at dozens of bars and brothels.*

FOLLOWING PAGES: Like fallen clouds, patches of fog cling to Queensland's Daintree National Park. Daintree's splendid rain forest setting earned its inclusion as part of the Wet Tropics World Heritage Area.

To help restore a mangrove forest bulldozed by a developer, environmental crusader Margaret Thorsborne plants a seedling at Oyster Point on Hinchinbrook Channel. Scientists warned that without the stabilizing effect of mangroves, the shore would erode and a vital habitat for wildlife and fisheries would be lost. Opposition to putting a huge resort and marina adjacent to world heritage areas prompted the Queensland government to introduce a bill that would give it unprecedented powers to prevent undesirable coastal projects. The federal government has approved the construction of the resort under strict environmental guidelines; the controversy continues.

Serpentine creeks vein a mangrove wilderness in Hinchinbrook Island National Park, Australia's largest island national park. Behind the barrier beach, salt-tolerant mangroves grow on prop roots that foster a rich habitat for marine life. A domain of diverse landscapes, the park protects rain forests, savanna woodlands, crystal streams, and granite mountains. Wallaman Falls, on the mainland, leaps from an escarpment 30 miles inland and plunges a thousand feet to the Herbert River, which flows into Hinchinbrook Channel.

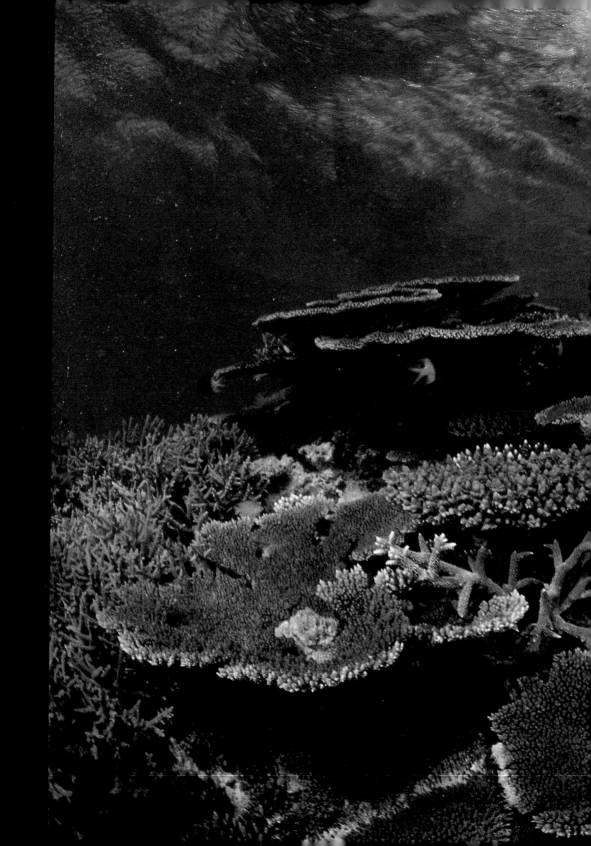

GREAT BARRIER REEF

*Photographed
by David Doubilet*

In the warm shallows
of the Coral Sea, in
waters so clear they
almost vanish, minute
members of the animal
kingdom have created
a colossal complex of
barrier reefs, coral cays,
and limestone islands
known as Australia's
Great Barrier Reef.
Constructed over the
eons by tiny coral
polyps, the reef
stretches 1,250 miles
along the Queensland
coast and is the largest
structure on earth built
by living beings. Each
polyp of stony coral
builds a cup of
limestone around itself.
A polyp dies and
decays, but its rocky
base remains,
and another polyp
builds on it.

Plates and branches of
Acropora *corals form an
undersea garden near
Lizard Island.*

*FOLLOWING PAGES:
Feathery tentacles sprout
from the polyps
of a gorgonian sea fan.*

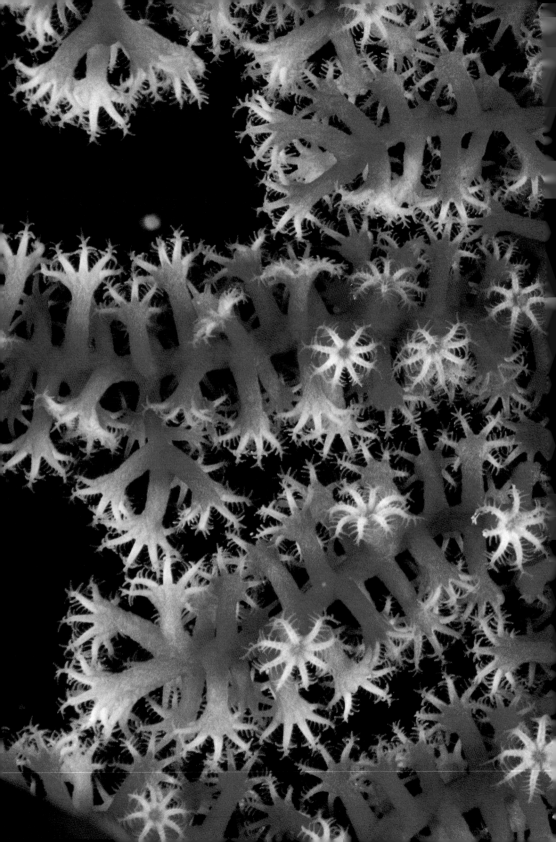

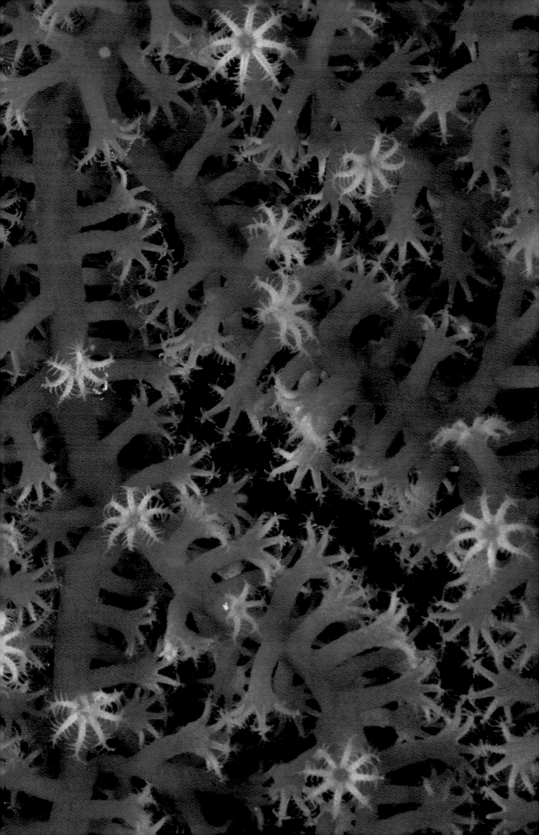

Immune to the venomous stings of a sea anemone, clownfish (opposite) in the northern barrier reef find safety and sustenance among the creature's tentacles. On the lookout for danger as well as prey, a goggle-eyed blenny (above) peers from a coral crevice off Heron Island; a harlequin tuskfish (below) bares a mouthful of blue fangs.

FOLLOWING PAGES: Waiting to go ashore on Raine Island to lay her eggs, a green turtle will deposit them in deep holes she excavates in the sand with her flippers.

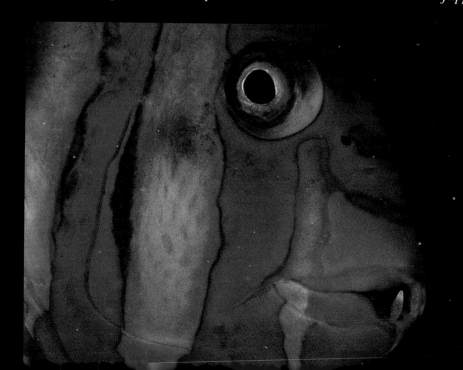

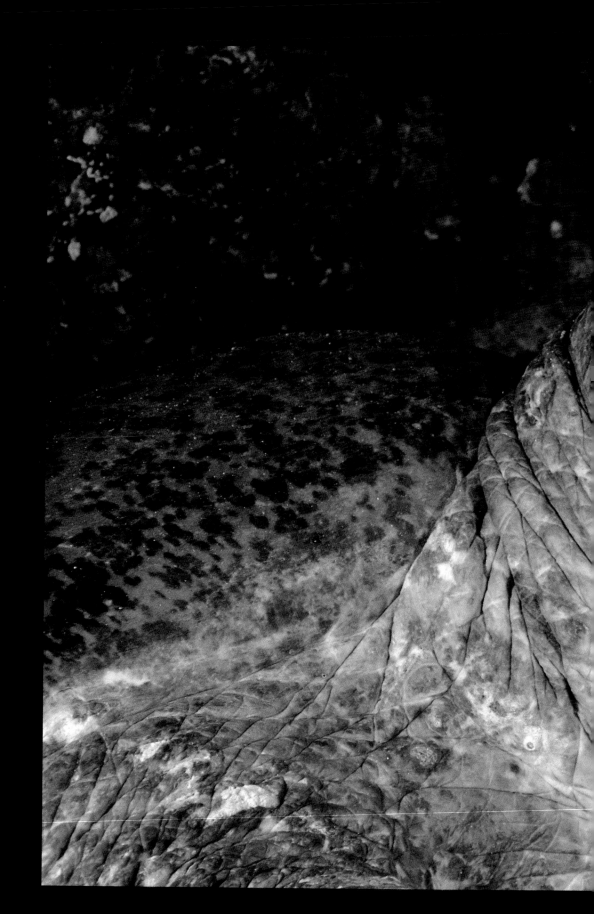

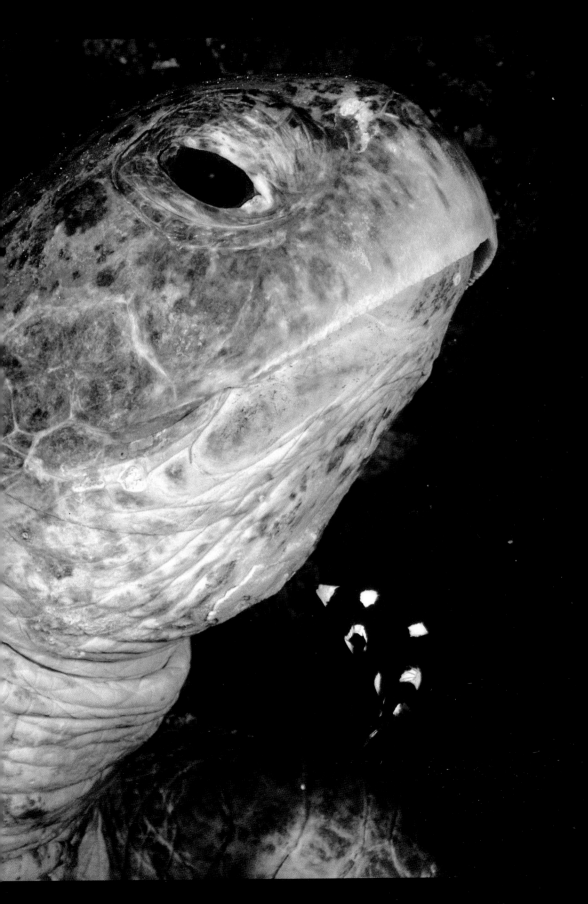

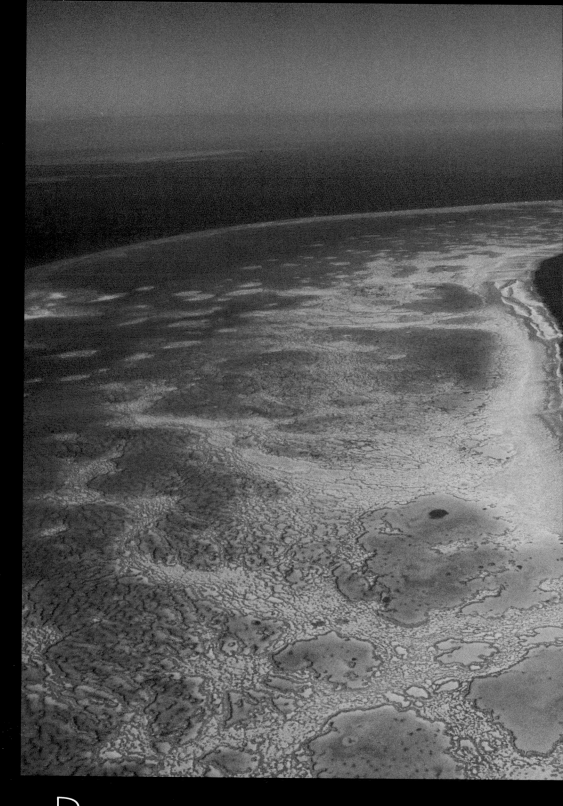

$\mathcal{D}$*eep blue of an ocean channel divides turquoise shallows between Hook and Hardy Reefs*

near the Whitsunday Islands. Coral colonies punctuate the water in an aerial view.

Marooned offshore, wave-cut pillars known as the Twelve Apostles—all that remain of earlier headlands—attest to the power of the sea along Victoria's southwestern coast.

FOLLOWING PAGES: Sydney's landmarks, the span of the Harbour Bridge and the parabolic shells of the ultramodern Opera House, bracket the view from an open-air café.

THE HERITAGE COAST

Photographed by Sam Abell

Surfers in Australia have learned to change their clothes on the beach without giving away any secrets. They wrap a beach towel around themselves, then wiggle and squirm, and off come their street clothes; then they wiggle and squirm some more and on go their trunks. The towel is discarded, and the job is done. On chilly days, many also don skintight wet suits. The suits zip up the back, and the surfers have attached a foot-long strap to the zipper, so they can reach back over their shoulders and zip themselves up. It looks like they're hoisting themselves by their own suspenders.

They're a single-minded and determined bunch. They're in such a hurry to get into the water that they run from their cars toward the waves, carrying their surfboards. Rain or shine, any time of day, you'll see them out there, rising and falling in the swell, waiting for the right wave to come along. At 9:30 on Christmas morning I found them already in the waters off the town of Margaret River in Western Australia. In their glistening black wet suits they reminded me of predators of some sort, sea lions maybe, waiting for prey. They disappear as they drop down the slope of a swell, then rise into view again, their backs turned to the shore, peering out to sea, waiting and watching, all in a cluster.

They've named a city after themselves on the east coast of Queensland south of Brisbane—Surfers Paradise. It may be heaven to surfers, but it's hell to anyone trying to drive through. Combining the worst of Fort Lauderdale and Malibu, with a little Gatlinburg thrown in, Surfers Paradise is solid development, with high rises obscuring the beach and fast-food restaurants and four lanes of traffic turning the air blue with greasy smoke. My Fielding guidebook said, "You can do just about anything in the Surfers area that humans have devised to amuse other humans."

This string of beaches, the so-called "Gold Coast," reaches from a little south of Brisbane to the New South Wales border. In 1824 the state's governor, Sir Thomas Brisbane, had a penal colony established where Redcliffe now is, at Moreton Bay, but the colony failed. The soil was poor and seeds died; convict-workers developed scurvy and dysentery. Medicine ran out, and there was not enough ready lumber for building. In 1825 Governor Brisbane had the whole settlement picked up and moved 27 miles up the Brisbane River, where the city flourished.

It's the city where I saw Kangaroo Szechwan on a menu and ate in the Bow Thai Restaurant. A taxi driver pointed out a longshoremen's pub in the dock area. "Brisbane has a new law requiring beer to be sold from aluminum kegs," he told me, "but the longshoremen thought it ruined the taste and went on strike, demanding wooden kegs in their pub. So an exception was made for them. It's now the only pub in Brisbane with wooden kegs. But it's come to be such a trendy and swish place that the long-shoremen don't go there anymore."

South of Brisbane, in New South Wales, Cape Byron sticks a thumblike promontory out into the ocean. It's the easternmost point of the Australian mainland. A lighthouse sits high atop it, and from it you can look down onto the sea, where a school of bottlenose dolphins may be lazing just offshore. They move independently yet together, like elements of a Calder mobile. On rocks along the beach below, surfers have painted "Locals Only."

A sign offering surfing instruction to backpackers caught my eye in Byron Bay, so I looked up Lester Brien, who runs what he calls "surfaris" along the coast. Backpackers—or budget travelers—who want to learn to surf come to him for lessons, either a quick three-hour course out in the bay or a week-long trip by bus between Byron Bay and Sydney. "Most of my customers are from other countries," Lester told me. "If Australians care anything about surfing, probably they've already learned. As for the foreigners, in three hours I can't really teach them to surf, but they get wet and have a lot of fun.

"The thing about surfing is, it's fun while you learn. Probably more than any other sport. Right from the first minute, you're involved in a friendly environment, and you're having fun. Surfing's a very hard sport, though. The difference is, you don't have a stable surface. And most foreigners don't seem to understand wave movement the way young Aussies do. I guess it's something we're born with."

It was on a beach in 1879 that Australia's system of national parks began. As Sydney had grown and become overcrowded, officials were concerned about public health. Children were dying young, and the citizenry needed a place for public recreation out in the fresh air. About 17,000 acres were set aside south of Sydney, and an official attempt was made to duplicate London's Hampstead Heath. Trees were planted, deer brought in, and exotic birds and fish released. Pavilions, guest houses, and camps sprang up. For 76 years its name was simply the National Park. It became the Royal National Park in 1955.

Australia now has something like 800 national parks, though many are tiny—mere islets or patches of bush. Many are coastal, jewels hung on the long necklace that is the country's shoreline. Yuraygir National Park, just north of Coffs Harbour, stretches along some 43 miles of coast and inland about 3 miles, protecting beaches, headlands, rivers, and lagoons. Backing up from the coast, wetlands merge into woodlands, which in turn become forested hills. About 25 miles north of Port Macquarie, Hat Head

National Park attracts visitors interested in photography, biology, and birding. Behind dunes fronting the sea, its 15,925 acres are covered with grasses and creepers, then banksia and tea-tree scrubs, swamp sedges and wet heaths, forests of eucalyptus, and finally wooded ridges. Hawks, falcons, and sea eagles soar overhead, hunting.

Cities dot the coast along here as well as parks. Port Macquarie and Newcastle began as many Australian cities did—as penal settlements for troublesome prisoners who needed to be separated from others. A sadistic commandant at Port Macquarie, who loved to have prisoners flogged, boasted that he "would make the Deaf to hear, the Dumb to speak, the lame to walk, the blind to see, and the foolish to understand" through flogging. Newcastle's first settlers were convicts sent in the early 1800s to mine a vein of coal three feet thick that ran near water level.

Of Sydney, the British actor Robert Morley once wondered, "Why didn't they call it Bert?" In fact it was named for the British home secretary, Viscount Sydney, when it was established as a penal colony. The First Fleet, in 1788, brought 775 condemned prisoners to Australia, as well as a contingent of marines and wives and children. Supplies included 40 wheelbarrows, 747,000 nails, and 250 women's handkerchiefs. The first suicide occurred soon after the fleet landed: Dorothy Handland, probably the oldest person in the settlement, a perjurer, hanged herself from a gum tree. Throughout the 1790s, an average of a quarter of a million strokes of the cat-o'-nine-tails were administered each year.

Sydney today, as it clings like a barnacle to its magnificent harbor, is one of the world's most beautiful and cosmopolitan cities. Once almost entirely of British stock, Sydney now—thanks to a more liberal immigration policy in recent years—has ethnic enclaves from around the world. Of monuments, memorials, and statues, there are many, but perhaps none nicer than the memorial near Circular Quay to Matthew Flinders, an early English seaman who navigated all around Australia in the early 1800s, charting its coast. Alongside his memorial is a smaller one to his cat, Trim, with an epitaph that Flinders wrote: "To the memory of Trim, The best and most illustrious of his race, The most affectionate of friends, Faithful of servants, And Best of creatures."

A map of New South Wales south of Sydney looks crowded and confusing, with networks of highways and clusters of towns, but it turns out to be wonderfully rural, with large chunks of countryside between towns. In places, scrubby pine forests with red-dirt logging roads reminded me of Georgia.

I drove along the south shore of New South Wales and Victoria toward Adelaide, along a rugged and beautiful coast. At many headlands, fishermen stood on surf-splashed boulders at the water's edge, casting their lines into the ocean. Surprisingly, I later learned, they were engaged in one of Australia's most dangerous sports: Every year some 15 people are swept to their deaths while rock fishing in New South Wales alone.

In Eden I stopped at the Killer Whale Museum, which had been recommended to me, and browsed among displays of whales and whaling. In the early days, when whalers worked the waters off Eden, a pack of killer whales patrolled its Twofold Bay and actually helped the whalers. They herded baleen whales into the bay one at a time, then held the animal there until the whalers arrived. Their reward was the tongue and lips of the harpooned whale. On a wall by the skeleton of "Old Tom" I read: "As leader of the pack, Tom would swim to the whaling station at Kiah Inlet, leap out of the water and splash about until the whalers launched a boat, then lead the way to where the whale had been rounded up by the pack. In his impatience, Tom sometimes seized a boat's harpoon line to slow a whale down and even towed boats holding the towrope in his teeth." Tom died in September of 1930, and not a single killer whale showed up the next season.

Even more astounding—and more unbelievable—was the story of what the museum called "A Modern Jonah." In 1891 a huge sperm whale, harpooned but still alive, surfaced and smashed a boat full of whalers to pieces. Two men were missing. The whale surfaced about sunset and died. The whalers winched it to their vessel for processing and, as they worked on it, noticed a rhythmic movement from the whale's paunch. They cut it open and discovered one of their missing comrades, James Bartley, unconscious but alive after 15 hours in the belly of the whale. "Its digestive juices had permanently bleached his skin a deathly white. He lost his hair and was nearly blind. For two weeks he was delirious, and it was a month before he could tell how he'd fallen into the whale's mouth, felt the huge teeth grate over him as he slid down into its throat, then its stomach, in which live fish were flapping." He lived another 18 years.

As Cape Byron is the easternmost point of Australia's mainland, Wilsons Promontory is its southernmost. A high granite peninsula 125 miles southeast of Melbourne, the "Prom"—as its friends call it—juts into the cold waters of Bass Strait. More than 75 miles of hiking trails crisscross its 120,000 acres. Eucalyptus and banksia woodlands clothe the Vereker Range, which rises in the center. About 120,000 years ago the promontory was an island, but since then sand has built up and formed an isthmus.

A similar isthmus connecting the promontory to Tasmania was inundated by a rise in sea level about 15,000 years ago. In the early 1800s sealers and whalers worked the waters off the promontory, and logging, tin mining, and grazing were part of its past. In World War II commandos trained here. It was reserved as a national park in 1898 and became one in 1905.

At dusk, large roadside meadows have the feel of African plains. I strolled through one just as day was ending. Kangaroos and emus peacefully fed, and a wombat scratched himself. Australia's wombat population is suffering from a mange that is killing many and tormenting many more.

At rest, kangaroos lie on their sides, like cats. The emus have knobby knees, skinny legs, and a stately strut. They look a little like dust mops. Nearby, a flock of 25 or so sulfur-crested cockatoos, a kind of parrot, chortle in the grass and dance around one another. A tourist in tight pants tried to feed a kangaroo from a plastic bag of garbage. Another kangaroo came up behind her and gave her a swat, which sent her scurrying back to her car.

A tree that grows here—the lilly-pilly—has given its name to a gully and a footpath through it that I walked one afternoon. High in a blue gum tree, a koala was sleeping in a fork. Crimson rosellas, as tame as pets, came and sat on the trail at my feet. People evidently feed them. They did everything but climb up onto my shoes. They are a kind of broad-tailed parrot and are bright red and blue with distinctive cheek patches. Retracing my route later in the afternoon, I found the koala awake but sluggish. It stared down at me in a dim fashion, then climbed a little higher in the tree, reached up, and pulled down a small branch. It began studiously and slowly munching its leaves.

A ferry from Sorrento across Port Phillip Bay to Queenscliff bypasses the urban tangle of Melbourne and delivers you to southwestern Victoria. It was peaceful and comfortable on the ferry, a huge boat with dozens of people and automobiles. I had a coffee and sat eavesdropping on my fellow passengers.

"I've got almost flat feet," one told a companion.

A man said to his wife, "It wouldn't surprise me if, in the end, Mum changes her will and leaves everything to Jim."

"No, she won't!" said his wife.

Americans are largely charmed by the Australian accent— though in Australia, of course, it's the Americans who have the accent. To me, Australians sound faintly comic no matter what they're saying. And they do wonderful things with nouns. Schoolchildren are "schoolies." Truck drivers are "truckies." Surfers are "surfies." Boaters are "boaties." A big he-mannish tour leader in Queensland offered to stop the bus so we, his passengers, could take some "pickies." Woolworth's is "Woollies." Chickens are "chooks," so there's a fast-food outlet called Mr. Chook. Australians call their swimming trunks "bathers." Men really do say, "G'day, mate." An announcer on a classical radio station, praising the ethereal, fluty sound of a British male chorus, said, "And they're all blokes, even those high voices."

Food is called tucker, and in Hobart I saw a sign advertising Chinese Tucker. In Darwin I heard a man say to his friend, "Me Mum always told me, 'Don't say yairs, say yiss.'" Sometimes the accents get pretty thick. One day, seated comfortably on a beach, leaning back against a post, reading, I was addressed by an Australian couple walking by. He said, "Gryte plyce to ryde."

At a lodge west of the Prom, I had a two-minute conversation one morning with an elderly man—my host called him "an old ocker"—and I didn't understand a single word he said. I was talking about the weather—about the clouds in the sky and what might happen later in the day—and I hope he was talking about the weather, too.

Driving off the ferry at Queenscliff, I picked up the Great Ocean Road, a narrow, winding route to Mt. Gambier—about 340 miles away in South Australia. The road was built between 1919 and 1932 as a memorial to World War I veterans and also to provide jobs during the Great Depression. About 3,000 former servicemen were employed on the section between Cape Patton and Anglesea. From Anglesea to Apollo Bay the route was cut out of the cliff faces of the Otway Ranges and hugs the coast. The Great Ocean Road runs through some of Australia's most beautiful mountain and coastal scenery—and along some of the country's most renowned surfing beaches. Each Easter contestants from all over the world come to Bells Beach near Torquay for surfing competitions. On good days, swells move shoreward in sets of four or more, forming perfect surfing waves perhaps 10 to 13 feet high. In the 1981 World Surfing Championships, waves were nearly 20 feet high. I visited the beach on a cold, drizzly morning and found surfers hard at work—bobbing on distant swells and waiting, always waiting.

Later that morning I met a group of young bicyclists laboring up a steep hill in the drizzle, their eyes fixed on some distant goal. The road wound back and forth, up and down, with occasional breathtaking views of rocky headlands and surf battering itself to foam against them. Little resort towns wait every few miles.

At Apollo Bay, named for the sloop *Apollo* by its captain, who sheltered here from gales in 1846, the road curves inward for a bit to get around and through Otway National Park. This 30,000-

acre park takes in most of the Otway Peninsula and includes spectacular coastlines and rain forests. Mountain ash grows here, the world's largest flowering plant and, in height, second only to California's redwoods. The average height of a mountain ash is 165 to 260 feet, with a few reaching more than 300 feet.

The section from Cape Otway to Port Fairy is called the Shipwreck Coast, for the scores of vessels that have come to grief here. About 1,200 ships of all types have wrecked in this 90-mile stretch, about 13 ships for every mile of coastline. Matthew Flinders thought he "had seldom seen a more fearful section of coastline." The worst year was 1858 when seven ships, some filled with emigrants heading for Victoria's newfound goldfields, were lost on this coast.

There is a 19th-century prayer, reputedly uttered by children living near the coast west of Cape Otway. "Dear God, Bless mummy and daddy and please send us another wreck soon."

A lighthouse has stood on 300-foot cliffs at the tip of the cape since 1848, in an often futile attempt to keep ships away from the rocks. Its lantern was built in London and hauled through the surf to the site of the lighthouse. It had 21 parabolic reflectors, each with a wick burning sperm whale oil. The rotating lantern gave a single three-second flash every 53 seconds, which could be seen 13 miles out to sea.

Nearby Melba Gully State Park is named for the famous Australian diva, Dame Nellie Melba. It's in one of the wettest parts of Victoria, with annual rainfall of more than 80 inches, so vegetation is lush and green, with tree ferns overhead and low ferns and mosses alongside the trail. Walk in from the parking lot and there's an immediate sensation of cool darkness. A breeze rustles the trees, and a little stream rushes along the bottom of the gully. A gust of wind in the treetops made me look up in time to get a face full of water the gust had shaken down. The park's chief feature is Big Tree, a gnarly, 300-year-old behemoth of a species of eucalyptus called Otway messmate. Daffodils bloomed along the path to the parking lot.

Along the Shipwreck Coast winds and waves roar in from the Indian Ocean south of the continent, an area known locally as the Southern Ocean, and carve the limestone coastline into sea stacks, arches, and cliffs. One windswept headland was bathed in moonlight when Matthew Flinders sailed by in 1802, so today it's still called Moonlight Head.

In Port Campbell National Park, which encompasses the coastline between Princetown and Peterborough, the highway runs through sand dunes and low coastal heath. Many short side roads carry visitors to the coast, where wind and waves of the Southern Ocean have sculpted dramatic forms. Rugged sea stacks called the Twelve Apostles, some more than 200 feet tall, stand in the surf just offshore from the cliffs, survivors of the soft limestone coastline as it retreats from the battering waves. The wind was so fierce when I stopped I couldn't get my jacket on. It stood straight out horizontally from the back of my head. I had to get back in the car to get into it. A big bus full of Japanese tourists and a small bus of Americans were having the same problem. Waves crashed against the Apostles as if they were determined to batter them to pieces, and clouds of spray looked like a fog bank rolling in.

Farther up the coast the waves have succeeded in doing some damage. What once was London Bridge is now London sea stacks; a mighty arch that connected the headland to the mainland collapsed into the sea in 1990, stranding two terrified visitors on the seaward end. A helicopter had to come and hoist them off.

Mutton Bird Island, near the mouth of the Loch Ard Gorge, is a rookery for some 200,000 muttonbirds, or short-tailed shearwaters. The wreck of the *Loch Ard,* snapped in two and buried on either side of the reef that sank her in 1878, lies just 200 feet from the mainland on the southeast side of the large stack. En route for Melbourne from Gravesend, England, the *Loch Ard* was a three-masted square-rigger with a crew of 36 and 19 passengers. Capt. George Gibb, just 29, was in command. He had expected to sight Cape Otway, their first land in a thousand miles, on June 1. But sightings taken the day before were inaccurate, due to a thick haze obscuring the sky. At four in the morning on the first, the haze lifted and high pale cliffs were sighted just a mile ahead. The lookout aloft could hear breakers.

Captain Gibb hoisted more sail and tried to turn the ship back seaward, but it was too late. He ordered the anchors dropped, but they dragged on the sandy floor. The *Loch Ard* backed stern-foremost onto Mutton Bird Island, its yardarms striking the island's cliffs as waves rolled the ship. Grinding on the reef tore the bottom out, and battering against the cliffs sent the masts and rigging crashing onto the deck. The *Loch Ard* quickly sank.

Only two people survived, the ship's apprentice, Tom Pearce, and a young passenger named Eva Carmichael. Tom swam through the surf to a small beach in the gorge and was resting there when he heard cries from the sea. He swam out and found Eva clinging to a spar, and brought her ashore. They were at the base of cliffs 300 feet high, their only refuge a small cave. After a short rest, Tom managed to climb the steep cliffs and find help from two astonished sheepherders. Four bodies were found. They were buried at the top of the cliffs in coffins fashioned from pianos salvaged from the wreck, and there they remain. Eva remembered Captain Gibb speaking to her as the ship sank: "If you should be spared ever to see my dear wife, tell her that I stuck to the ship to the last, and went down with her like a sailor!"

Romantic imagination of the time insisted there be a romance between Tom and Eva, but evidently one never developed. Eva returned to Ireland, and Tom went back to sea, where his troubles continued. His next ship, the *Loch Sunart,* sank off the Irish coast in 1879, and his son, Tom Jr., was drowned when his ship was wrecked off Kangaroo Island in 1905. Another son was killed in World War II.

Another wreck, if it could ever be found, might cast light on the early history of Australia. Called the "Mahogany Ship," after the supposed material of its deck, the wreck was first reported on the beach west of Warrnambool in 1836. Elderly Aborigines living nearby claimed it had been embedded in the sand there all their lives and spoke of "yellow men" who once had lived among them. It might have been a Spanish or Portuguese ship, locals speculate, and could date back to the 1500s. Searches were made for it late in the 19th century, early in the 20th, and as recently as 1992, all unsuccessful.

Port Fairy, originally named Belfast, once was second only to Sydney in the busyness of its harbor. Whalers and sealers used the beach for rendering their catches, and the town was formally laid out in 1843. Most of the construction was done in the 1840s and 1850s, and the town hasn't changed much since. More than 50 buildings are now classified as historic by the National Trust.

I had some soup and an enormous sandwich for lunch in one of them, built as the post office in 1865 and used as borough chambers from 1882 to 1990. I worked off my lunch strolling up and down blocks with the town's "Historic Walks" map in front of me. Mills Cottage, built on Gipps Street sometime around 1840 for John Mills, harbormaster, was constructed of materials shipped from Tasmania. It may be the earliest building still standing in Victoria. The community has produced maps, too, that will take you to vantages overlooking different shipwreck sites. At least 30 vessels were wrecked around Port Fairy between 1836 and 1876.

The charming little city of Mount Gambier sits atop a restless and unstable base: volcanoes and sinkholes line a coast that has been submerged many times over the last 40 million years by fluctuating sea levels. The sea laid down huge beds of limestone, which now are fissured by tunnels and caves. The volcanoes were still erupting as recently as 1,400 years ago. They appear in the legends of local Aborigines. Mount Gambier has several crater lakes in its center, one of them called Leg of Mutton Lake for its supposed shape. All are beautiful, with pure waters popular with snorkelers and divers. Blue Lake is a rich cobalt blue in late November and remains so for Australia's summer months, evidently because calcium bicarbonate and calcite crystals precipitate out faster when the water is warm.

My favorite stop in Mount Gambier was at the Lady Nelson Tourist Information Interpretive Centre. Here there is a full-size replica of the *Lady Nelson*, the ship that first charted this coast in 1800. The exhibit includes a figure of her commander, Lt. James Grant, who speaks! A recording somewhere in him tells of the voyage and life aboard ship, while lights in the vessel rise and fall at areas he's discussing. Sailors sway gently in hammocks, and among the supplies stored in the hold a rat scurries into the darkness. It was aboard the *Lady Nelson* that its next commander, Lt. John Murray, discovered the great bay now called Port Phillip, the harbor of the modern seaport of Melbourne.

Coorong National Park is 37 miles of barrier dune and inlet reaching toward Adelaide. Its warm, shallow waters breed fish and waterfowl for fishermen and birders. At its north end, the sluggish Murray River often can't reach the sea without help from bulldozers, which make a path for it through the dunes. Fierce winds off the Southern Ocean bend beachside paperbarks and ruffle the feathers of stately pelicans.

At the head of the inlet, near present-day Adelaide, Matthew Flinders in 1802 came upon two westbound French ships at anchor in what he named Encounter Bay. *Le Géographe* and *Le Naturaliste* were charting the coast and the waters between Australia's southern coast and Tasmania, an important though rough shipping route that, if used, reduced by several weeks the passage from England to Sydney. Their commander, Capt. Nicolas Baudin, was already referring to southern Australia as *Terre Napoléon*. To forestall the French, settlers were quickly sent from England to found Melbourne, and by the time Adelaide was founded in 1836 the French were long gone.

I avoided Adelaide, as I had Melbourne, by sticking to the coast. The rural and peaceful Fleurieu Peninsula juts out into the Indian Ocean south of the city. I drove down its length to Cape Jervis at the tip, past flocks of sheep on hillsides; they stood so still they looked like Paleolithic boulders. From Cape Jervis I could see, off in the distance, the gray profile of an island. Flinders discovered it in 1802 and, because its bush was thick with kangaroos, so named it—Kangaroo Island. Another ferry would take me there.

arly morning anglers cast from shore at Byron Bay, one of the resort towns along the north coast of New South Wales, where beach follows beach almost continually for 360 miles.

PRECEDING PAGES: A joyous announcement displaces a butcher shop's daily list of specials in Byron Bay, a mecca for those seeking perfect surfing waves and a relaxed lifestyle.

Still water and lichen-encrusted granite create a landscape as spare and serene as
a Japanese garden at Whale Rock in Victoria's Wilsons Promontory National Park. Nearby,
in the Prom's fern-mantled Lilly Pilly Gully, a blue-cheeked crimson rosella (above) perches
on a dead eucalyptus. Grasses camouflage a wombat (below) as it forages for food.

FOLLOWING PAGES: Lush pastures carved from rain forest provide rich fodder for cattle in
Victoria's Otway Ranges, but patches of wilderness remain, alternating with farmland.

Blustery seas assail Victoria's Shipwreck Coast, a graveyard for some 1,200 vessels that foundered in storms spawned hundreds of miles away. Ashore, wind and waves have sculpted a landscape of cliffs, sea stacks, and arches stretching more than 90 miles.

"Dark, wet and gloomy," an early visitor thought Tasmania, but the Roaring Forties that lash the island also clothe it in lushness. In farms and towns, English echoes resonate.

FOLLOWING PAGES: Ruins of Port Arthur, site of Tasmania's most infamous prison, rise through midday mist. Here convicts from England were housed—and brutally punished.

TASMANIA

Photographed by Sam Abell

On a map Tasmania looks like an afterthought, a chunk of land left over after the rest of the continent was formed, tucked out of the way in an empty part of the ocean down toward Antarctica. It's like a punctuation mark, or the dot on an *i*. About the size of West Virginia, and representing less than one percent of Australia, the island sits off the foot of the east coast, separated from the mainland by the fierce waters of Bass Strait. The island was discovered by accident in 1642 by a mariner who was lost. Abel Tasman's instructions from the Dutch East India Company were to sail into the Southern Ocean to latitude 54° south and then to sail east until he found the mysterious southland—Australia—that had been reported there, thereby mapping "the remaining unknown part of the terrestrial globe."

Unlike later mariners, who seemed continuously to be bumping into Australia, Tasman missed it completely. Too far south, he sailed between the mainland and Tasmania, which he spotted and named Van Diemen's Land for his patron. Explorers visited with some regularity. A party of Frenchmen astonished a group of Aborigines in 1802 by singing "La Marseillaise." François Péron reported, "Hardly was a verse finished than loud cries of admiration broke out...."

Such happy relations would not last. By the late 1880s there were no full-blooded Tasmanian Aborigines surviving at all. They had been replaced by another class of suffering souls: convicts transported from England. When the American Revolution cost the English their North American repository for convicts, they began shipping them to Australia, first to Sydney and then, beginning in 1803, here to Van Diemen's Land. By 1820 the island was a vast jail.

And a crowded and hellish one, at that. Historian Robert Hughes calls it "another pit within the antipodean darkness, a small hole in the world...which would in due time swallow more than 65,000 men and women convicts." Supervision was lax, food was scarce, punishment was frequent and brutal. Many transportees were hired out to free settlers as virtual slaves. By 1836 half the 43,000 residents of Van Diemen's Land were convicts.

An early governor, George Arthur, believed "a convict's whole fate should be...the very last degree of misery consistent with humanity....The most unceasing labour is to be extracted from the convicts...," he wrote, "and the most harassing vigilance over them is to be observed." He had a new prison built for felons convicted of committing further crimes and named it for himself—Port Arthur, now Port Arthur Historic Site. It's on the Tasman Peninsula southeast of Hobart. A thin spit of land,

Eaglehawk Neck, offered the only access to the site and was so narrow a line of dogs could guard it against escaping prisoners.

Today the ruins of the prison at Port Arthur are so beautiful it's easy to forget what horrors took place here. About 40 buildings—some picturesque ruins, some restored—dot the lush, parklike grounds. A slow drizzle the day I visited was turning the grounds even greener, and many visitors were clad in white plastic ponchos handed out by the park, in sizes ranging from Extra Large Daddy to Tiny Toddler. They were patterned with stylized black arrows that once had been used to identify the prisoners' clothing, so the visitors drifted through the misty grounds like the uniformed ghosts of former convicts.

The four-story penitentiary, built as a granary in 1842 and badly damaged by fire in 1897, had a look of gothic ruins—its roof missing, its brick walls partly gone. It could accommodate 657 men in cells and dormitories. Wooden walkways lead through several levels of the ruins; from the upper, you can look down into the former cells, as narrow, deep, and dank as wells.

Prisoners were kept occupied during their stay. They built ships, logged, farmed, quarried, and even mined coal. A "model" prison was added to the site in 1852, where the latest theories of enlightened incarceration were practiced. Prisoners were kept in solitary silence except when attending church services; when they moved around the prison they were masked. Hymn singing was their only vocalization. They were meant to continually reflect on their crimes and struggle to reform. Many went mad.

Transportation of convicts from Britain to Van Diemen's Land ended in 1853. For many at Port Arthur, the end came just offshore on a sad little island called the Isle of the Dead. An early clergyman selected it as a burial site because it "would be a secure and undisturbed resting-place, where the departed prisoners might lie together until the morning of the resurrection." Less than two acres in area, the island became the burial ground of more than a thousand people. Convicts—mostly nameless—were buried in graves marked only by mounds of dirt.

Through the fog, the island looms in the distance. A tourist boat goes there several times a day, a five-minute ride, and I went along. As the drizzle fell and the trees dripped, tour guide Ashley Law, under a big yellow-and-black umbrella, urged us to keep together on the wood-chip path. "Even on the path we're presumably walking over bodies," he told us. We huddled together, 20 or so of us. A little girl, barely a toddler, was wearing a perfect miniature sou'wester, yellow and shiny. Ashley read us part of a poem about "the unremembered dead...who died amidst their chains." Gusts of wind sent clouds of mist across the crowd.

There were only a few gravestones, some erected for prisoners after their deaths by their families, others for freemen or soldiers who had died while on duty at Port Arthur. Australia's first published novelist, Henry Savery, is buried here. His stone, erected by an Australian writers' group and a local newspaper, was inscribed, "businessman, convict, forger, and author." Another stone bore a poem: "Affliction sore/Long time I bore /Physicians were in vain/Till God did please/That death should ease/Me from my pain."

We moved on through the drizzle, big drops from trees occasionally thumping on our umbrellas. "Over here is George Britton," Ashley said, pausing by a weathered stone. "He had one of the longest terms served at Port Arthur. He spent 28 years in prison, from 1832, and served solitary confinement 604 days, hard labor 5,909 days—which works out to 16 years—and received 766 lashes. He died while working in the quarry, from stooping over a blasting charge when it went off. They called it an accident, but I think it was probably suicide, don't you?"

It's a place of punishment still, I found. On the boat back to the mainland, a toddler ran in tears to his mother. "What's wrong, sweetheart?" she asked. "Daddy gave me a smack," he sobbed.

With transportation of convicts halted, Port Arthur began a decline. In the 1870s it was closed and stripped of everything moveable. Tourists began arriving soon after.

The most dreadful of the penal settlements was on the west coast at Macquarie Harbour, where I continued my circuit of Tasmania. Incorrigible prisoners were sent here as further punishment to work harvesting timber and coal. Their only escape route was across great tiers of interior mountains or on the occasional ships that visited the site. Prisoners were housed on Sarah Island, in the harbor, and early each morning taken ashore to cut timber. Giant Huon pines, prized for use in shipbuilding, grew thick in the area, but harvesting them was brutally difficult. Men worked with primitive tools, felling the trees and sliding them to tributaries of the Gordon and Franklin Rivers, where they were formed into rafts. The convicts worked up to their chests in freezing water, lashing the logs together and then wrestling them ashore on Sarah Island, where they were used in the shipyard. The logs were sawn over pits and shaped into vessels ranging from dinghies and whale boats to a 226-ton bark, in all 113 craft between 1823 and 1833.

Until the 1970s, the town of Strahan on Macquarie Harbour was Tasmania's only port on the west coast. Tour boats cruise daily from the town to Sarah Island, and on another cool, misty day I rode along. Our old and historic wooden boat chugged through gray water, under a gray sky, rimmed by gray mountains.

Not much remains of a place that was once so busy. Narrow walkways and boardwalks took us from site to site—the penitentiary, the bakehouse, the blacksmith shop—and past signboards. "Read it to me," a woman said to her husband, "so I don't have to put my glasses on."

The last ship built on Sarah Island—the 121-ton brig *Frederick*—was involved in a daring escape. Convict James Porter and several of his mates overpowered guards and crew and put them ashore, then sailed the *Frederick* across the Pacific to Chile. They settled there, took up their trade of shipbuilding, and several even married and had families. Four, including Porter, were eventually recaptured, however, and returned to Van Diemen's Land, where they were charged with piracy. Parker successfully pleaded a novel defense. Since the *Frederick* had never been formally commissioned, he argued, "it was canvas, rope, boarding and trenails, put together shipwise—yet it was not a legal ship: the seizure might be theft, but not piracy."

Back aboard our tour boat, we had tea and cookies while the boat steamed slowly up the Gordon, perhaps Tasmania's loveliest river. It forms high in the King William Range. Of the giant stands of Huon pine that lured the lumber industry here, only a few youngsters grow along the banks of the river today.

A bitter environmental battle was fought here in the 1970s over the proposed damming of the Gordon and the Franklin Rivers. Developers and the Tasmanian Hydro-Electric Commission wanted the dam for electric power; environmentalists wanted the region left alone. Both sides lobbied hard. The issue came to a head with the Blockade, which ran from mid-December 1982 until early March of 1983. Thousands of protesters poured into the region for one of the greatest environmental protests ever seen in Australia. Flotillas of "rubber duckies" blocked barges at the dam site, sit-ins stopped bulldozers, people chained themselves to fences and equipment, and access roads were blockaded. Hundreds were arrested. The Australian Labor Party came out in opposition to the dam and was swept to power in a major federal election, which helped spell the end of the dam. The region is now included in a giant world heritage site that protects nearly two million acres of western Tasmania.

Tasmania is so small you can drive all the way around it in a few days, but I took my time and moseyed north from Strahan up to the far northwest corner, which pokes bravely out into the frigid waters of Bass Strait. From Smithton I drove west to Green Point early on a peaceful Sunday morning and watched the beach come to life. Campers emerged from sleeping bags and shook them out. A mother set out breakfast on a picnic table. Children in tiny wet suits were already headed for the water. Two fishermen arrived in a Jeep. Seaweed undulating in the swells looked like animals in the water. Willie wagtails hopped along the rails of a wooden fence, looking down into the grass for bugs. A pelican standing on a rock a few yards from shore stared with seeming disapproval at the children swimming, and a cormorant on a rock farther out spread its wings to dry.

East of Smithton, the north coast of Tasmania is punctuated by a curious geologic feature called The Nut, an ancient volcanic plug that Matthew Flinders in 1798 described as a "cliffy round lump in form resembling a Christmas cake." Attached to the mainland by only a narrow isthmus four-and-a-half miles long, it rises straight out of the ocean to nearly 500 feet.

A cable car runs to the top from the little town of Stanley, so I climbed aboard for a breezy ride. Stanley welcomes you with a sign reading "Tasmania's Tidiest Town," and it certainly looked that way from high overhead. I passed over people walking to the top of The Nut on a trail so steep they were on tiptoe. It's called The Nut Track, because only a nut would attempt it.

Stanley's near neighbor to the east is Rocky Cape National Park, a small park with quiet beaches and hillsides dotted with eucalyptus. A stubby lighthouse stands on the very tip of the cape. I was alone there with the wind and the gulls. Pink granite boulders were scarred with the movement of the ages.

A sandy footpath led a few hundred yards to North Cave, which was used by Aborigines for thousands of years. A tiny lizard scurried away as I walked through the scrub, and little swallows abandoned their nests in a flurry of panicky, shrieking flight as I entered the cave. A European surveyor and a party of convict workers found the cave and a group of Aborigines here in 1827. I sat in the mouth of the cave for a bit contemplating what life must have been like here. Not bad, in many ways. A steady breeze kept the flies away. The ocean, with its limitless supply of food, was nearby. Scrubby brush for firewood was plentiful.

Archaeologists believe the cave was first occupied about 5,500 years ago. A 1965 dig yielded bones of fish, marsupials, seals, and a variety of shellfish. Stone tools from a midden above the cave came from quarries some 45 miles to the east and west.

Tasmania's Aborigines were quickly and brutally eliminated by the early settlers. According to Robert Hughes, they were "shot like kangaroos and poisoned like dogs, ravaged by European diseases and addictions, hunted by laymen and pestered by missionaries, 'brought in' from their ancestral territories to languish in camps." Within 75 years of European contact the Tasmanian Aborigines were virtually extinct.

The drive along Tasmania's northwest coast toward George Town puts the cool blue waters of Bass Strait at one elbow and lush green farms and forests at the other. Little towns all seem to have a white sand beach and a marina.

At George Town, the long finger of Low Head reaches out into Bass Strait, its tip punctuated by the red-and-white Low Head Lighthouse, built in 1888, and a pilot station. In early days, pilots had to row some two or three miles out to ships to guide them to their berths, often against a flood tide. The maritime museum here houses many artifacts of piloting, including a terrific working model of a semaphore station.

I sat for a while at a tiny wildlife sanctuary alongside the highway in George Town, watching black swans feeding in the shallow river. With their heads underwater they looked like black boulders that would suddenly sprout long necks and heads. A sea gull strolled by, up to its ankles in the gentle surf. There was no friendliness in its cold yellow eyes.

In the agricultural land east of George Town, several unusual crops crowd the coast. Fields of poppies bristle with signs that read, "Prohibited Area. Keep Out. Trespassers Prosecuted." I felt like a criminal just stopping to take a picture. Each bulb looks like a miniature greenish pumpkin with a tiny fringed cap on top.

Processors extract opiate alkaloids from the dry capsules of mature poppies. Seeds and oil are used in cooking, but Tasmanian poppies are grown mostly to produce codeine and morphine, used in a variety of painkillers. Only farmers holding contracts with registered manufacturing companies and licenses from the Tasmanian government are allowed to grow the crop.

Nearby were some of the most beautiful fields I had ever seen—row upon row of lavender plants, with Tasmania's gentle green mountains in the background. The Bridestowe Estate lavender farm was established by an Englishman, C. K. Denny, and his family in 1921. They planted lavender seeds from the European Alps. Patricia Mountney showed me around and explained the workings of the farm. "This part of Tasmania has soil and climate similar to southern France, where lavender grows naturally," she said. "That's why it does so well here. Ours is the only source of perfumery lavender outside of Europe."

It was only about a week before harvest time, and the fields were in full, magnificent bloom. "The plants are grown in contoured rows to prevent erosion," Patricia said. "There's plenty of rain here, so we don't have to irrigate, and there are no pests of lavender in Tasmania, so there's no fencing. The plants live about 15 years, but they don't provide a decent harvest until they're 3 or 4 years old."

Patricia took me to the distillery where the plants are processed. "The lavender is pressed into bins and lowered into vats hot with steam, where it's heated until the buds burst open. As the vapors rise and pass through water-cooled pipes, a liquid trickles into a glass beaker—lavender oil. It takes 250 kilos of flowers to yield three liters of oil."

Driving in Tasmania is easy—not much traffic, clearly marked roads and highways, lots of friendly little towns to stop and explore. Though the highways are hazardous to animals. Tasmanian devils, real animals with some similarity to the cartoon character, are fierce but no match for modern automobiles: their furry corpses dot roadsides all over the island.

Freycinet National Park is a mountainous 29,479 acres on the east coast with a cuddly town—Coles Bay—nearby, and a comfortable lodge for pampering visitors. I devoted a couple of days to being pampered, going for walks with the naturalist-ranger, watching wallabies watch me—they scratch, sniff the air, then bound off in a ridiculous manner—and exploring on my own, one day to the Friendly Beaches.

The walk from the parking lot led along a sandy path, edged by tall green scrub, full of the chirps of invisible birds. The sound of surf led me on. It was windy on the beach, and bright—even with sunglasses, the glare from the white sand was harsh. I could look a couple of miles or so in either direction and see no one: I was alone on a beautiful beach on a sunny afternoon in a national park. Pale green breakers were rolling in; they formed a kind of parenthesis before falling on their faces. Wisps of spray were being blown off their crests. Bits of dry seaweed skittered across the beach, looking like animals of some kind. Cold-eyed seagulls were plentiful, and I marveled, not for the first time, at the amazing number of them that walk with a limp. A big white-breasted sea eagle flapped laboriously by, into the wind.

It's easy to sit alone on a beautiful beach, I thought; there never seems to be a good reason to leave.

I completed the circle of Tasmania back in Hobart, the state's tiny capital. Only about 190,000 people live here. Whaling and sealing helped Hobart grow in its early days, and it became an important port for exporting wool. It was declared a city in 1842. It has the friendliest cats in Australia.

I happened to arrive during the finish of the yearly Sydney–Hobart yacht race and watched a few of the graceful boats reach their moorings in Sullivans Cove. An American yacht, *Sayanara,* was the winner, and its decks were busy with smug-looking young men scrubbing and airing sails and gear.

I strolled from the harbor to Battery Point, so-named for the guns here that once protected the harbor. Or such was the plan. Actually the troops were more enthusiastic about drilling and wearing impressive uniforms than battle. The Hobart Town Volunteer Artillery Company was formed in 1859. Before it practiced firing, an officer would visit all the houses behind the battery to warn them to open their windows or have them broken by the blasts, which, according to a sign nearby, "was the only damage the Volunteers and the batteries ever inflicted." A committee in 1865 concluded that the Volunteers were "next to useless," and the unit was dissolved. Hobart was left defenseless, but no one ever attacked.

On Salamanca Place, a street of old warehouses, shipping offices, and storerooms, the city spreads a marketplace each Saturday morning, filled with food, crafts, used clothing, books, and antiques. The crowd was elbow-to-elbow when I was there. I heard a woman call to her husband, "Steven! Have you got the kids?" "What?" said Steven. There were wool products for sale, bakery items, jewelry, pottery, hats, and handbags. People were eating French fries out of paper cups. A toddler wore a T-shirt reading: "I'm A Little Tasmanian Devil." The smell of incense wafted through the air. I accepted a free sample of hot Tasmanian mustard on a cracker. People pushing baby carriages caused serious traffic jams in the crowd.

Down Montague Lane I came upon a courtyard with picnic tables, buildings on three sides, and a sheer cliff—part of an old quarry—on the fourth. The Round Earth Company was staging its version of "The Ship That Never Was," the story of James Porter and the convicts who stole the *Frederick* from Sarah Island and sailed it to Chile. A small but friendly crowd of 30 or so was watching. It was a jolly performance filled with broad humor and audience participation. Four actors, dressed in prisoners' stripes, enacted the story, narrating as they went along. During the performance, they put together a wonderful 50-foot replica of the *Frederick,* complete with gaudy sails and a tiller. Audience members were given paper sacks to blow up and pop, simulating musket fire. Others, with water-filled spritzers, sprayed the actors during a storm at sea. Since there was no cat available to play the ship's cat, a small terrier was borrowed from a spectator.

Tasmania, it appears, has come to terms with its brutal past and tucked it comfortably into the world of make-believe, slapstick, and farce—probably the best place for it.

*P*eace reigns on Hazards Beach in Freycinet National Park; a tree's shadow strains
seaward (opposite), and tannin from nearby tea trees tints shallows copper (below).
Dunes along the beach are rich with ancient Aboriginal shell middens, reminders
of a people virtually exterminated in Tasmania by disease and warfare
in just a few decades. Probably no more than 4,000 Aborigines existed in Tasmania.

PRECEDING PAGES: Tenacious still life clings to a cliff in Freycinet. Tasmania devotes
nearly a third of its area to a world heritage site and to other forms of parks or reserves.

Poppies blanket a hillside in northern Tasmania. Growers must be licensed to raise

the crop for pharmaceutical companies that produce painkilling codeine and morphine.

Lush ferns frame two-level Russell Falls in Mount Field, Tasmania's first national park. In 1885, 300 acres around the falls were proclaimed a reserve; it was enlarged and named a national park in 1916. Glacial tarns and lakes feed several waterfalls here, in Tasmania's most popular park.

FOLLOWING PAGES: Softly blooming lavender curves toward distant hills. Climate and soil similar to southern France's, where lavender grows naturally, led to the introduction of the crop in 1922.

SOUTHERN SEAS

*Photographed
by David Doubilet*

Where cold waters of the southern Ocean flood a wide, shallow continental shelf and bump against a warm landmass, undersea life blossoms. Nutrient-rich currents of cold Antarctic water rise to the surface here, making this Australia's most productive sea area. Fishermen find abalone, lobster, prawn, and tuna in these teeming southern seas. Atop the food chain sits one of nature's most fearsome predators—the great white shark. In the 2,000 miles from Australia to Antarctica's ice, fierce storms whip the chilly waters. British navigator Matthew Flinders charted this southern coast in 1801-1802.

*Attracted by a chum of
tuna entrails, a great
white attacks near
Dangerous Reef.*

*FOLLOWING PAGES:
Graceful sea lions
dance above a grassy bed
in sun-shot waters
of Spencer Gulf.*

Crazy shapes and colorful forms populate the waters off Australia's southern coast. Small but deadly, a four-inch-long blue-ringed octopus (top) expands and contracts pigment sacs in its skin to flash a vivid warning; most venomous of all octopuses, it can kill an adult human. A three-inch-long pinstripe squid (left) uses its sharp beak to inject prey with toxins from its salivary glands. Largest of the world's hundred cuttlefish species, the giant cuttlefish (opposite) is found only in Australian waters. The three-foot-long cephalopod seizes crabs and shrimp with sucker-tipped tentacles and holds them fast with shorter arms.

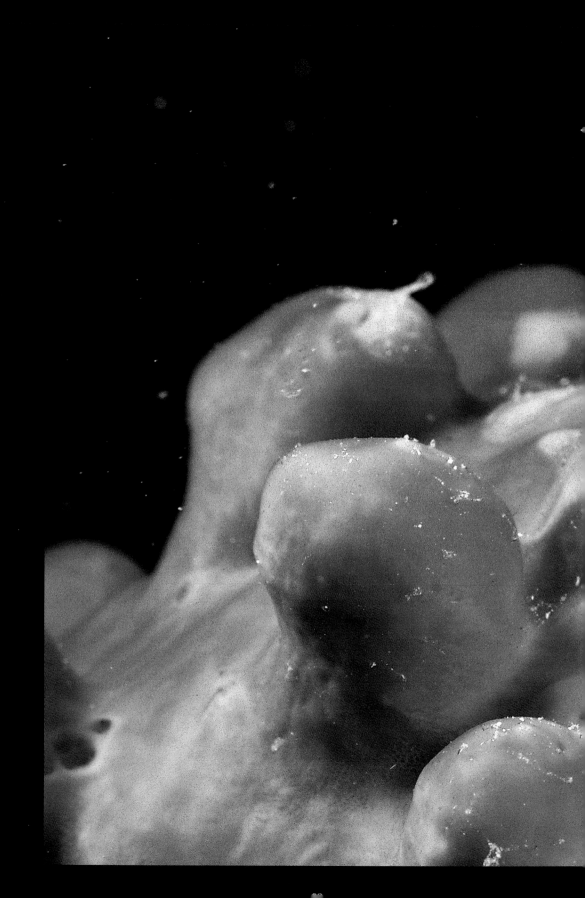

Solitary fisherman faces the surf on a lonely beach east of Israelite Bay.
Crystallized carbon streaks the sand pink; distant sandhills rise white and mirage-like.

FOLLOWING PAGES: Like a dog herding sheep, a shark guides migrating salmon
into coastal shallows off Baxter Cliffs, on Western Australia's southern coast.

SOUTHERN EXTREMES

Photographed by Sam Abell

I t being an island, I naturally arrived on Kangaroo Island from the sea, as did the peripatetic Matthew Flinders before me. I came by ferry; he discovered the island from aboard his ship *Investigator* in 1802. He and his crew dined on the gentle and plentiful kangaroos, which he noted were darker, longer-haired, and more heavily built than the kangaroos of New South Wales. He named the island for them, and today they're recognized as a subspecies of the western grey kangaroo. In 1803, a year after Flinders' visit, French navigator Nicolas Baudin sailed around the island, giving many places the French names that survive today: Cape du Couedic, D'Estrees Bay, Cape d'Estaing. That same year American sealers built a 35-ton schooner named *Independence* in a lagoon at the east end of the island. The site now houses a resort town named American River, though it isn't a river and there are no longer any Americans there.

Kangaroo Island, with 2,800 square miles, is Australia's third largest island, after Tasmania and Melville Island, and was first settled by whites in 1836. Enigmatic original inhabitants left archaeological evidence behind, but no one knows when or why they left. Today the island is home to about 4,500 people, who farm and fish and cater to tourists. They're torn between embracing the tourist industry, for the income, and keeping their island a secret. It has been called a miniature Australia: It has beaches, mountains, and forests; kangaroos, cockatoos, and wallabies; even a tiny desert. It has never had rabbits, foxes, or dingoes, so has escaped the ecological damage of much of the mainland. Kangaroo Island looks a lot like the rest of Australia once did. It boasts South Australia's first cemetery and its oldest fruit tree, a mulberry planted in 1836. About a quarter of the island enjoys some sort of official protection.

It retains its small-town atmosphere. In Kingscote one day, strolling through the downtown area, I came upon an old dog tied to a lamppost. He looked like he'd seen his share of battles—his ears were scarred and his eyes were a little out of focus—but he gave me a grin and a wag of his tail. Nearby, striding back and forth in a busy but distracted sort of way, was a white cockatoo. He, too, looked like he'd seen better days. His feathers were dirty and ruffled, and he walked with a bowlegged stagger. I noticed their presence and went on about my business. Half an hour later, when I returned, they were still there, and I realized with a start that they were pets, waiting patiently for their owner.

Like all Australian shorelines, Kangaroo Island's is thick with shipwrecks. The first was recorded in August 1847, and since then more than 60 vessels have been lost here. One of the most beautiful was *Loch Vennachar*, which sailed into the cliffs of the island's west coast in 1905. A signboard outside my hotel, the Ozone Seafront, told of another wreck, in 1908, when the master of the *Robert Burns* mistook a white light on the hotel for a navigation beacon.

One day I set out with Ken Grinter, a naturalist-guide on the island, to a seal slide on the south coast. We drove past fields of bright yellow canola and grazing sheep. "There are 1.3 million sheep on Kangaroo Island," said Ken, "and 4,000 people, so I hope we never do anything to make the sheep mad."

We drove for one hour, then left the vehicle and walked for another along a narrow sandy track above the cliffs of the south coast. A fierce wind beat at our backs as we wound up and down and back and forth through the bush. Ken was educated as a chemist and worked for ten years in a salt mine in Western Australia. Now, in addition to guiding on Kangaroo, he manages the post office in American River. He pointed out wildflowers as we walked along—salmon correa, a small shrub with red flowers; a bush pea whose blooms looked like bacon and eggs; a velvet bush with tiny pink flowers.

Fresh burrowings alongside the track were the work of an echidna. We came upon it eventually, its face in the dirt, busily digging. It looked something like a porcupine, though its spines are not barbed. Its protective coat made me think of a clump of chrysanthemums. We kept downwind of it, walked softly, and got within a few feet of the shy creature. It would poke its snout, the size and shape of a little finger, into the dirt and hold it there for a few seconds, using receptors in its tip to detect electrical signals given off by worms and ants. It looked like it was taking the ground's temperature. When it found something, it would dig furiously with its front feet.

Ken whispered, "When they're threatened, they can dig with all four feet, so they sort of sink down into the sand with nothing but their spines showing. Not much can harm them, though on the mainland introduced foxes can sometimes turn them over and get to their soft bellies." Echidnas can live to be 50 years old; among mammals only elephants and people have longer life expectancies. Our echidna finally got wind of us and ambled off into the bush.

At the misnamed seal slide, sea lions emerge from the sea to sun themselves. Many laboriously heave themselves up steep dunes to sunny spots out of the wind, where they sprawl and snore. Returning to the water, they slide down the dunes in a charming and playful way. We sat for a bit and watched a couple of them wake from their naps and head out to sea. A pup, flippers flailing wildly, tobogganed down, fishtailing and skidding.

Australia's cockatoos are large parrots with powerful bills and crests on their heads. All screech and congregate in large, noisy flocks. One of the rarest is the glossy black cockatoo, a subspecies of which is believed to survive only on Kangaroo Island—in a population that has been dwindling over the years and is in danger of flickering out altogether. A lot of people on Kangaroo Island are involved in the effort to save the glossy black cockatoo. They're beautiful birds, a rich black in color. The females have tails barred in yellow, orange, and red, with yellow flecks on the sides of their heads. The males have brilliant red-and-black tails.

But it's the old story: development destroying habitat.

"They're so specialized they don't make things easy for themselves," said Terry Dennis over dinner one night in Kingscote. Terry is project supervisor of an official Australian effort to study and save the glossy black cockatoos of Kangaroo Island. "They eat only cones from drooping she-oak trees, and the trees are being cleared for development. They nest only in the hollows of old-growth gum trees, which are also popular with possums and bees. They're very long-lived birds, but they only reproduce themselves a couple of times in their life. They raise just one young at a time and invest in it very heavily."

There are an estimated 180 birds left on the island. Bryon Buick, a fifth-generation islander, donates some of the proceeds from a poster he painted to helping save the bird. To him, "the glossy black has got character and an intelligence high above a lot of other things. He seems very wise. And gentle. He's a character! But every creature's got a reason for being here. If there were just 180 of anything left, I'd feel the same way." He calls Kangaroo Island "a magic little place."

Belinda Hannaford, whose house on the north coast overlooks a magnificent bay and beach, has planted a thousand she-oak trees just this year and has plans for many more. She runs a B&B, so is very aware of the difficulties of balancing development with protecting the island's fragile environment. Belinda is critical both of backward farmers and overzealous tourist proponents. "You go to meetings and everyone has wonderful ideas, and nothing happens," she says. She has populations of glossy black cockatoos on both sides of her, but none yet on her property. "It takes a few years for the trees to mature," she says.

Both wooden and PVC nest boxes have been placed throughout the island. The cockatoos love them, but so do brushtail possums and bees, both of which displace the birds.

I saw another famous Australian bird while en route to Flinders Chase National Park, which covers most of the west end of the island and is named for our old friend Matthew Flinders. A huge wedge-tailed eagle was trying to lift roadkill too heavy for itself, flapping mightily to get airborne while two big black crows pestered it.

Flinders Chase covers some 185,000 acres and features open woodlands and eucalyptus forests, mallee scrub and heathlands. There are no introduced predators, so the wildlife is peaceful and plentiful. Along the park's south coast are a couple of features that beckoned me: Admirals Arch and Remarkable Rocks.

Admirals Arch was down a sloping, hard-surface pathway, thick with beefy Germans puffing their way upward; then down wooden steps to an observation platform near the arch at the base of the cliffs. Waves were crashing in, thundering through the narrow opening and sending spray flying, but in quiet pools among the rocks, seals played and swam, peering up out of the water or snoozing on spray-blackened boulders. Their lithe bodies slid through the surging surf with perfect effortlessness.

Remarkable Rocks are just that: huge, wind- and rain-sculpted boulders precariously balanced on a gigantic granite dome. "Remarkable" is the only word that occurs when you see them. I loitered in the parking lot and eavesdropped on tourists who would invariably say, "Those rocks are really remarkable!"

With the growing population of Adelaide just to the northeast and the juggernaut of burgeoning development and tourism looming over it, Kangaroo Island is holding its breath as it tries to find a balance between development and despoliation. Bryon Buick hopes it will be developed "with charisma and style."

Across Spencer Gulf to the northwest of Kangaroo Island, at West Point, begins the giant indentation in the southern edge of the continent called the Great Australian Bight. It reaches 680 miles from West Point to Cape Pasley in Western Australia. Its waters, the Southern Ocean, are renowned for the ferocity of their storms and their heavy seas. There are safe anchorages and ports scattered throughout the bight, but much of the coastline consists of steep cliffs—which *Australia: the Rough Guide* calls "absurdly melodramatic"—more than 300 feet high.

Heading west from Ceduna, you're faced with a long drive. There's a lone signpost in the center of town, pointing west, labeled "Perth." It's along here that you see a famous yellow highway sign warning of a trio of creatures: camels, wombats, and kangaroos. It marks the beginning of a completely treeless run of hundreds of miles where services are very limited.

The Yalata community, not quite halfway along, was settled by Maralinga Aboriginal people after they were forced off their traditional lands in the 1950s so the British could conduct atomic bomb testing there. Today the Maralinga sell permits to tourists to cross their land to the Head of Bight, the best place to see southern right whales as they calve between May and October. You can stand on precipitous cliffs and look almost straight down into the water where mothers and calves cavort, feed, and rest.

Back from the coast is the Nullarbor Plain. Nullarbor is a corruption of the Latin for *nullus arbor*—no tree. There are scattered sheep stations here and not much else. It never rains on the plain, and the rivers are the shortest in Australia, seldom more than 30 miles long.

This coastline, too, was surveyed in 1802 by Matthew Flinders.

Flinders was born in Lincolnshire in 1774, joined the British Navy in 1789, and two years later served under Captain Bligh on his second voyage to Tahiti. In 1795 Flinders came to Sydney.

In 1798-99 he and George Bass sailed the 25-ton *Norfolk* around Tasmania, surveying the coastline. Flinders gained the patronage of Sir Joseph Banks to survey the entire coast of Australia and left England in 1801 in command of *Investigator.* He surveyed uncharted sections of the east coast, the Gulf of Carpentaria, and Arnhem Land in the north. He continued around the continent, but returned to Sydney without having completely surveyed the northwest and west coasts. Nonetheless, the work he had done earned him a reputation as one of the greatest hydrographers of all time.

Flinders visited my next stop, but didn't name it. That had already been done by a Frenchman, Admiral d'Entrecasteaux, who sheltered offshore and named the bay after his ship, *L'Esperance.* Flinders came along ten years later, mapping and charting, and named a few features: Lucky Bay, Thistle Cove, the Barrens. In 1826 a military presence was established here, primarily to serve the many ships—especially whalers and sealers—that called, and also because Britain feared annexation by the French. Today the town serves an agricultural area, but fishing and tourism are also important industries.

I arrived in Esperance after dark, in a plane two hours late. "They only have two arrival times," said the man at the Avis counter, "late and later." At my motel, a friendly tomcat wanted to come into my room, but was forbidden by a stern owner.

I got a small plane to take me for a look at the western beginnings of the cliffs of the Nullarbor on a day of puffy clouds and clear air. From the air, the ocean's deep blue turns to pale green as it approaches shore, then turns to the white of sand on miles of beaches. We flew among huge sand dunes, turning and twisting. Dark streaks of minerals line the sand, and little points of vegetation try to poke through. Suddenly the cliffs of the Nullarbor emerge from behind the dunes and intersect with the ocean. They're narrow layers of limestone of different earthy hues with white froth at the base. In many places, the cliffs have lost chunks of themselves, which are piled up in pyramids at their base. On the top, scrubby bush runs perfectly flat for as far inland as the eye can see. Dirt tracks, which pass for roads here, look as if they were made with a pizza slicer, running straight to the horizon.

In pale shallows at the base of the cliffs, a school of small sharks all swim along in the same direction. The plane skims along just a few feet above the water, lower than the tops of the cliffs.

Esperance briefly made world news in July of 1979, when Skylab, the orbiting American space station, fell to a fiery death. Pieces of it rained down upon the Esperance area in a bizarre storm that left residents partly angry and partly bemused, but gave the municipal museum a terrific display. In a glass case 20 or so feet long there is a model of Skylab, newspaper clippings and photos, and bits and pieces of the spacecraft: a circuit board, insulation fragments, part of a freezer, a door hatch. One subhead reads, "People in Esperance are angry at the size of Skylab fallout being found near town." Another, under a photo of people in a field examining debris, reads, "Space Giant Dies Roaring." A map shows the path of the descent across Western Australia. There is a photo of Stan Thornton, who found the first fragments and thereby won a trip to the U.S. to display them.

Harold Hardwick takes tourists on trips through the outback and along the beaches of this part of Western Australia—to Cape Le Grand National Park and beyond to Cape Arid National Park and the Nullarbor Plain. I rode along in Harold's Land Cruiser for a day of exploration. We drove eastward from Esperance along the beach, across hard sand and through soft dunes. At rocky headlands, Harold put the vehicle in four-wheel drive. We charged up one huge headland, a couple of hundred feet high, and it was like driving up the side of a basketball. In the dunes, we left the Land Cruiser and sat down gingerly on small wooden snowboards to toboggan wildly down the slopes and reach the bottom breathless and with mouths full of sand.

As we drove, Harold told us how even an experienced bushman such as himself can find himself in trouble in this unforgiving part of the country. On a trip a few weeks earlier he had agreed to take along, at reduced prices, a couple of young backpackers in exchange for their help cooking and stowing gear, which is lashed to the top of the vehicle. He had four people from Melbourne on a five-day trip to the cliffs. On the last day of the trip they stopped at dusk to camp at Toolinna. A backpack was missing from the vehicle's roof. Harold drove back and found it, but used up several hours' worth of fuel. Not to worry, he thought, he had a spare 20-liter fuel drum on top of the Land Cruiser. The next day he was horrified to find it was missing, too; it had evidently not been lashed on properly and had bounced off. There was not enough gas to get home.

Harold decided the only thing to do was walk the 50 miles to the Eyre Highway to get help. He and one of the tourists, Ian, set off at 2:00 p.m. carrying just a liter and a half of water, four oranges, and a flashlight. Soon they had blisters from the unaccustomed walking and stumbling in the night; to conserve the batteries, they used the flashlight only now and then. Their rests got longer, and the rutted tracks in the road got deeper. At 11:00 p.m., they reached a grassy plain, a landmark. They made a fire, and Ian slept. Harold sat and waited through the night.

In the morning each had an orange and a sip of water and set off across the featureless plain. They came to a line of trees, then another plain, on and on through the day. About noon Ian headed back for the vehicle, taking the remaining oranges, water, and the flashlight with him. In mid-afternoon Harold spotted a standpipe above a well he remembered from previous visits. The water was three feet from the surface, covered with green slime. Dead frogs floated in it. Harold dipped a stick into the water to moisten his lips and tongue. There was a line of trees in the distance he thought was the highway. He set off toward it.

Throat parched, peeling his tongue from the roof of his mouth, Harold staggered on. Hours later he realized he was on the wrong track and set off back to the well. Stumbling and staggering, he began to hallucinate. He finally found the standpipe, but couldn't locate the water in the darkness. He crawled around, sobbing, searching for it. Convinced he was dying, he set off another time, back and forth, helpless and confused. Lost, he wandered some more. At 2:00 a.m. he lay down, but the cold was so intense he couldn't sleep. He sucked pebbles to try to moisten his mouth. At dawn he realized he was on the wrong track yet again and finally found the well, where he wet his lips. He traveled 10 miles to the highway, crawling the last 50 yards, and lay by the side of the road where people would see him. At last he got a ride to the nearest town and safety. In all, he calculated later, he walked nearly a hundred miles on one orange and three or four sips of water. "Not bad for someone my age," he said.

Today Harold's Land Cruiser bristles with four different types of radios and their associated antennae.

One night Harold took me surf fishing on Rose Beach west of Esperance. Darkness arrived soon after we did, and the Milky

Way was like white sand spilled across the sky. The ocean churned and thundered at the edge of the beach, and waves came hissing up toward our parked vehicle. Harold erected a shelter and started a roaring fire. The fabled Australian "barbie" was soon sizzling—sausages, hamburgers, and steaks. The fishing gear I was using—a long, heavy pole and huge reel—weighed about a hundred times more than the only fish I caught, a four-inch sand whiting that was indistinguishable from a big minnow. We fished till 1:00 a.m. and got momentarily lost in the dunes going home, driving up and down and back and forth through featureless sand hills that looked the same from every angle. At 3:00 a.m. I crawled into bed. Not bad for someone my age.

Western Australia was the last part of the country to receive convicts, a contingent of workers at the military outpost that is the site of present-day Albany in 1826. The governor hoped the outpost would help civilize the area, overrun as it was by riffraff and desperadoes—depraved whalers and escaped convicts—who were settling along the southern coast.

Albany today bills itself as "The Town Where They Got It Right!" It boasts a laid-back mix of elegance and excellence without the snobbery and vulgarity of some other Australian tourist towns. I went shopping along steepish York Street for a sweater. The weather here on the south coast was turning chilly as the upside-down Australian seasons turned toward fall.

The woman who ran my motel, when I told her I was driving westward toward Cape Leeuwin, said, "Trees." She was certainly right about that. Some of the country's most magnificent forests lie in that 220-mile stretch. Forests of karri, marri, jarrah, and tingle trees remind you that you're not in Kansas anymore. Near Denmark, in the Valley of the Giants, about 100,000 visitors a year come to be dwarfed by red tingle trees that grow 200 feet high and have huge buttressed trunks that reach 15 feet in diameter. Precipitation of some 45 inches a year makes for lush forest. Just outside of Walpole I found the world's largest tingle tree—fire-hollowed, knobby and grotesque, like a haunt of hobbits or elves.

Names sprinkled along the coast here tell of a diverse past. Nornalup, D'Entrecasteaux, Chatham Island, and Cape Leeuwin speak of Aborigines, French, British, and Dutch in the area.

At the lighthouse on the tip of Cape Leeuwin, the cool waters Australians call the Southern Ocean meet the warm seas of the Indian Ocean. There is a fee of $3.50 to climb the 176 steps to the top of the lighthouse. "Whew!" said a young woman, halfway up. "They should be paying me $3.50 to do this." On top, the wind was howling, and whitecaps frothed both oceans. A marker, like a sundial, pointed toward the South Pole; there was nothing between us and Antarctica but water.

The first mariner to sight the southwest coast was evidently the captain of the Dutch ship *Leeuwin*—or Lioness—who left the name of his ship on this area in March 1622. Another Dutch ship, the *Elburgh*, recorded the first brief sighting of Aborigines on the cape in 1659. An armed shore party came upon three Nyungar Aborigines wearing kangaroo-skin cloaks, but the tribesmen fled when they saw the sailors, leaving behind spears and small axes. Several 18th-century mariners thought the cape was an island, and it was left to Matthew Flinders to set the record straight. He named this section of Leeuwin's Land "Cape Leeuwin."

By the late 1800s, pressure was being applied by insurance companies—including Lloyd's of London—for a lighthouse at the tip of Cape Leeuwin. The foundation stone was laid on December 13, 1895, and the structure was dedicated to the world's mariners. Limestone for the lighthouse was taken from a quarry nearby. Water came from an inland swamp and was carried through a wooden channel to a waterwheel, which turned the light. Today the wheel is stuck solid and turns no more.

One of the first workers at the lighthouse was a German, Felix von Luckner. He had run away to sea at 13 and ended as an assistant keeper at the light. Caught kissing the lighthouse keeper's daughter, he fled into the bush. After a period there, which he didn't like, he returned to Germany and joined the navy. He was decorated during World War I for sinking 14 enemy ships.

Even the lighthouse couldn't stop every mishap from happening. In 1910 the *Pericles*, bound for Fremantle and fully laden with passengers and cargo, came to grief here. The sea was calm, the day was clear, the light at Cape Leeuwin was in sight, and the captain, Alexander Simpson, was greatly experienced, having sailed some 2,060,800 miles in his career. Then the *Pericles* hit an uncharted rock. Captain Simpson ran up distress signals, but the lighthouse keeper didn't understand them. Passengers and crew abandoned ship. The *Pericles* sank three hours later.

Residents of Flinders Bay and Karridale as well as the lighthouse staff assisted the stranded passengers, and the Royal Humane Society gave awards to the lighthouse employees and presented the Anglican rector and his sister from Karridale with a gold watch and a gold brooch, respectively, for their part in rescuing and comforting survivors. Locals scooped up cases of apples and boxes of butter for weeks after the wreck. One little girl, who lived to be an old lady in Karridale, remembered her delight in finding amber beads on the beach, which she gave to her mother, and a beautiful hairbrush, which she kept.

Standing before the lighthouse at Cape Leeuwin on a cold and windy day, Kim McKeown said, "The chap who laid the cornerstone of this lighthouse was a great-uncle of mine." That would be Sir John Forrest, the first premier of Western Australia. Kim, retired now, lives in Margaret River, thought by many to be one of the prettiest regions in all of Australia. His parents built the Margaret River Hotel, which opened in 1936 and billed itself as the "premier pleasure resort of the south west."

Kim showed me around the Margaret River area on Boxing Day, the day after Christmas, far from the antifreeze and icicles of North America. December 25 in Australia is midsummer. Instead of sledders, surfers; in place of parkas, T-shirts; for Christmas dinner, not ham and turkey but prawns and crayfish.

Margaret River, a pastoral dairy, cattle, and timber region, has in recent years also become one of Australia's leading producers of premium wine. The climate, moderated by the adjacent Indian Ocean, seems perfect for growing grapes, and the lack of true winter means the vines are never fully dormant and are almost never damaged by frost. In less than 30 years, since the industry began here, some 50 vineyards and 30 wineries have been established, and roadside vineyards now are as common as wheat fields in Kansas.

Kim and I stopped at one—Leeuwin Estate—for a tour, and strolled among casks and pipes and barrels, the fruity scent of fermentation filling the cool air. The Leeuwin Estate has a beautiful outdoor amphitheater where big-name orchestras and other musicians come from around the world to perform on midsummer evenings.

At Hamelin Bay the skeleton of an old jetty reaches out into the water. Rails through the stands of majestic karri trees here once brought logged timber to the jetty for export. Heavy and water-resistant, it was used in building ships and piers. Stands of the big trees still line Caves Road south of Margaret River.

A shipwreck near here in 1876 is still talked about. When the *Georgette* ran aground in Calgardup Bay, Grace Bussell and her stockman Sam Isaacs rode their horses out into the surf to rescue survivors. They were taken to Wallcliffe House, Grace's home, and given shelter.

An even more famous shipwreck—one whose story involves murder and mayhem—would lure me farther up the long coast of Western Australia to Fremantle, busy port city at the mouth of the Swan River and the "Western Gateway to Australia."

"Energy and charisma," a friend says, Belinda Hannaford possesses in abundance. A longtime resident of 2,800-square-mile Kangaroo Island near Adelaide, Belinda is deeply involved in a land-care movement. Increasing development and tourism threaten much of the island—including the still-undeveloped bay Belinda's home overlooks (opposite).

PRECEDING PAGES: Burnished by dawn, cliffs of the Nullarbor Plain drop precipitously into the Southern Ocean. Here the continent draws back in a huge indentation— the Great Australian Bight—faced for nearly 700 miles with cliffs, many 300 feet high.

Heavily hunted for many years, sea lions find
refuge on Kangaroo Island. Rocky beaches along
southern Australia once teemed with fur seals and sea
lions. With few natural enemies, they were easy prey;
tens of millions were killed in less than 30 years.
The future of the island's glossy black cockatoo (above)
remains in doubt: Probably only 180 survive,
victims of shrinking habitat and competition from bees
and possums for nesting places in hollows of trees.

Tiny but tough, dune plants thrive in powdery sand of Nuytsland Nature
Reserve, a narrow strip of protected coastline that extends 250 miles from Israelite Bay
to near Madura, Western Australia. Silvery-green dune cabbages crowd clumps
of sea spurge (above). Coastal pigface (opposite) grows on beaches and sand dunes
from Israelite Bay to Geraldton. Nuytsland, at the western extremity of
the Great Australian Bight, got its name from Dutchman Pieter Nuyts, in 1627
the first European known to have sailed the waters of the bight.

PRECEDING PAGES: Like spilled paint, Lake Hillier splashes across Middle Island
in the Archipelago of the Recherche. High salt levels and low concentrations of nutrients
in the water of the lake encourage the growth of algae that stain the water pink.

onely sentinel on a remote coast, the lighthouse at Cape Leeuwin has warned shipping since 1896. For sailors and emigrants from Europe, the gleam of the lighthouse at 184 feet above mean tide level often offered the first glimpse of the continent. Visible for approximately 25 nautical miles, the limestone tower's electric light now glows with the intensity of nearly one million candles. Here, at the southwestern tip of Australia, the Southern and Indian Oceans meet, their waters roiled and confused. Lighthouse caretaker Kevin Rose (opposite) keeps watch on them.

Winged creatures of land and sea: A Brahminy kite (opposite) flies from the wrist of a handler at the Eagles Heritage Raptor Wildlife Centre near Margaret River. The center collects injured or orphaned birds from all over Australia and restores them to the wild. At Hamelin Bay patient gulls wait where tourists feed a hungry ray.

FOLLOWING PAGES: A familiar figure in Australia, a surfer rides a wave off Margaret River. Surfing competitions famous throughout the world are held on these beaches.

A limestone forest and setting moon loom above the dunes at Nambung National Park. Over time, wind and rain whittled these limestone formations into pinnacles.

FOLLOWING PAGES: Skyscrapers dominate Perth's business district on the northern bank of the Swan River; it divides the downtown and the city's suburbs.

THE GOLDEN WEST

Photographed by Sam Abell

remantle is one of those confusing Australian coastal cities with no square blocks, streets that unexpectedly become one-way, and abrupt dead ends. It's an aspect of the coastal cities I learned to recognize: They were built to conform to their waterfronts. So I floundered around for an hour or two, trying to find the Western Australia Maritime Museum, for I knew it told the story of the wreck of the *Batavia*, Australia's second oldest known shipwreck.

The *Batavia* was a merchantman of the Dutch East India Company that wrecked on the arid Abrolhos Islands some 275 miles north of here on June 4, 1629. The commander, the senior officers, and some of the passengers set off in two small boats to look for water, leaving 268 people behind. There followed three months of rape, murder, and debauchery as one faction of survivors made war on the other. The commander, instead of finding water, took a month to sail to Batavia—now Jakarta—and 63 days to return to the wreck, where he barely avoided being ambushed and killed himself by the mutineers. He found 125 men, women, and children murdered and the rest terrorized.

The bones of the *Batavia* moldered in obscurity for centuries until 1963, when a fisherman led divers to the wreck. Excavations during the 1970s recovered much material, which is now housed in museums in Fremantle and Geraldton.

In Fremantle, surviving hull timbers have been reassembled and artifacts such as coins and pottery displayed in glass cases. Most striking are the 137 shaped sandstone blocks raised from the *Batavia*. They puzzled archaeologists until someone fitted them together into an impressive portico intended for the castle in Batavia. Reassembled now in a somber room, the portal looks like something from a Cecil B. DeMille movie.

I visited the Fremantle Crocodile Park and noticed a sign advertising the Hard Croc Café. Croc farms and parks have sprung up in several areas of Australia, largely in response to the animals' near extermination by hunters. Both species—the so-called saltwater and the freshwater—were nearly gone from their range in northern Australia by the time bans on hunting were imposed between 1962 and 1974. There are now thought to be some 60,000 freshwater crocodiles in Australia and upwards of 60,000 salties in the Northern Territory alone.

Now farms around the country raise crocodiles commercially, both for their meat and more especially for their skins. The park in Fremantle had finches flitting around and just above the creatures' pools. "If they fly too low, the crocs'll have a go at them," said owner Don Wieringa. There were saltwater crocs penned there—including Bismarck and Rasputin. In Rasputin's pen was a sign: "Rasputin's my name, Gus to my friends. I'm the one with the big smile. I'm an amiable sort of chap. My mate thinks so too. I came from Wyndham in the northwest, but I'm happy here. See my new teeth growing?" As I watched, one of Gus's eyes slowly closed, then just as slowly opened again—a sinister wink.

I made it a point, whenever I talked with people who worked with crocodiles, to ask: "Do you dream about crocodiles?"— because they seemed to me the sort of beasts that might populate nightmares. Anna, at the Fremantle croc park, said, without a flicker of hesitation, "All the time. They sort of get into your head, and you can't get rid of them." When I later visited the Wyndham Crocodile Farm, I put the question to one of the workers, Mike Vance. "At first when I started working here, I had nightmares. I lived near the water, where there were crocs, and I dreamed about them getting into the house. A few times I woke up standing up in bed thinking there were crocs in my bedroom."

Mike Osborn, then manager of the Wyndham farm, couldn't shake hands with me when I first met him because his right hand was swollen and covered with big red stitches, the result of a bite a few days before. "I dreamed about crocs the night before I was bitten," he said, "but it's my first bite in a year." His wife, Anne, interrupted: "The first bite in a year that's *needed stitches.*" A six-footer had gotten him while it was being moved to another pen.

Fremantle's near neighbor to the north—Perth—has the west coast of Australia pretty much to itself. The nearest other state capital—Adelaide—is 1,315 air miles away. With Fremantle, Perth was host city to the America's Cup competition in 1987, just four years after the Australians took the cup from the U.S. for the first time in 132 years. The city gained momentary fame some years earlier when it turned all its lights on during the night of February 20, 1962, as a friendly gesture to astronaut John Glenn, who was orbiting the earth in his Mercury space capsule.

The black swans that caught the eye of an early Dutch explorer—he named the river the Swan—still attract visitors to Lake Monger in Perth. The city prides itself on being the friendliest and most relaxed capital in Australia, with perfect weather and sublime beaches. And it's the right size for a city, big enough to satisfy urban needs but small enough to explore comfortably. Because of its proximity to the Orient, Perth is the Australian city where I saw the most Asian faces while strolling around town.

North of the confused tangle of Fremantle and Perth, Australia's Route 1—a highway that runs virtually all the way around the country, clinging as closely as possible to the coast—once again brings order to chaos and makes circumnavigating the country easy. It carried me northward, toward the rugged and exotic northwest coast. Along the way, drivers pass scenic wonders. At the town of Cervantes, 150 miles north of Perth, tourists can chose a bus tour or can drive themselves ten and a half miles south to the Pinnacles Desert in Nambung National Park. In the desert country there, limestone spires rise dramatically from the bare sands.

Another 155 miles up the highway is the city of Geraldton, an important administrative center for Western Australia's midwest region and, because of its nearly perfect weather, a favored holiday destination of Perth families.

Geraldton was "proclaimed a city" during a visit by Queen Elizabeth only in 1988. Giant fig trees shade the entrance to the building that houses its maritime museum. Inside, I said to the woman at the desk, "What's the best thing in your museum?"

"It's all interesting," she said. "But you must watch our video. I'll rewind it."

"What's it about?" I asked.

"Oh," she laughed, "I can't give away the plot."

The video was about the *Batavia*. From it I learned, among other things, that the name of the islands the *Batavia* ran into— Abrolhos—is a derivation from the Portuguese for "keep your eyes open," an irony presumably not lost on the survivors. Glass cases held more bits and pieces of the wreck—pipes and pottery, bits of corroded metal and wormy wood. A map of the coast of Western Australia listed 785 shipwrecks; its border was black with their names, in tiny type.

It was a sunny Sunday morning in Geraldton, and the harbor was busy with people launching their little sailboats or supervising their children splashing in the surf. Everyone seemed to be 22 years old and to have perfect physiques and flawless tans. The harbor was alight with white sails bouncing and the heaving wakes of speedboats. One of them was towing things called ski biscuits, five at a time. They looked like large inner tubes, and each had a shrieking teenager sitting in it.

Nearby, a young father with a braided pigtail sat eating plums and watching his toddler daughter play in the sand. A yacht moored at the dock was named *Shenandoah*.

Shark Bay is the only place on the Australian coast I found that acknowledged perhaps the most fearsome legend of the country: that its shores are patrolled by evil, ravenous fish. The best Australian shark story I heard was about a man who dove off the pier in Fremantle and didn't even get wet. Statistics show that sharks killed 11 people in Australia from 1980-90; traffic accidents claimed more than 32,000 in that same period. On many beaches, nets protect the swimmers. But the shores are safer than the highways.

Shark Bay is one of Australia's most famous world heritage sites and is home to one of the world's last great surviving populations of dugongs. As many as 10,000 of the animals—ten percent of the world's total—live in Shark Bay. They feed on lush beds of sea grass growing in the shallows, and share the waters with humpback whales, turtles, manta rays, and, of course, sharks.

Worldwide, Shark Bay is one of only 13 places on a list of 469 world heritage sites that satisfies all four of the natural criteria for being listed. It has an "outstanding example" in each category: it has a life-form that demonstrates a major stage of earth's evolutionary history; it represents significant ongoing biological processes; it has unique or rare phenomena, formations, or features of exceptional natural beauty; and it has important habitats where threatened animals or plants survive. Other such sites in Australia include the Great Barrier Reef, the Tasmanian Wilderness, and the Wet Tropics in Queensland.

Shark Bay's premier attraction for tourists is the beach at Monkey Mia, where every day wild bottlenose dolphins come to be stroked, fed, and gawked at by humans. It is the only place in the world where wild dolphins regularly come into shallow water to interact with human beings. The dolphins started doing it back in the 1960s, when "Old Charlie" began accepting handouts from a local fisherman's wife. Soon other dolphins were accompanying Charlie to the beach, and they've been coming ever since. Today quite a sizable local tourist industry and resort are dependent on the animals showing up every day.

And show up they do.

In the morning, a crowd at the beach, standing and staring seaward, first alerted me to the arrival of the animals. Of the 400 or so dolphins thought to live off Monkey Mia, 6 are regulars. They live within about a six-mile radius of the beach. "The waters here are very rich, so they don't need to wander very far," Roger Syme, the resort naturalist told me.

Rangers are careful to feed the dolphins at irregular times and in insufficient amounts to satisfy them, so they never come at exactly the same time, and they always go away hungry. That feeding practice forces the animals to maintain their independence and their hunting skills.

On the beach that morning we are a mixed crowd—Australian, Japanese, German, French, British, and American—all lined up like a firing squad knee-deep in the water. The rangers are persistent in urging us to back up; if we go in too deep we'll alarm the dolphins. There are seven of them swimming slowly back and forth along our rank, just out of reach. They loll on their sides to peer up at us. You can see the whites of their eyes, which makes them look very human. They give a funny huff as they breathe. Travel writer Paul Theroux described some close up in the Mediterranean: "...a pair of dolphins appeared, diving and blowing, with that little grunt and gasp that all good-sized dolphins give out as they surface, as though to prove they are worried little overworked mammals just like you."

There are two regulars, Nicky and her four-month-old calf Hollikin. They're not fools; they know they're going to be fed. One nudges the leg of the ranger. The British woman beside me says, "Cheeky little bugger, innit?" Sure enough, another ranger appears with a bucket of fish, and we're all given the opportunity to hand a fish to a dolphin. Mine smiles at me as I bend down, showing what appear to be hundreds of tiny teeth, and takes the fish with an audible "snap." They entertain us for half an hour or so, then idly disappear.

Leaving Monkey Mia, I stopped for lunch at the Hamelin Pool Telegraph Station, a tiny, dusty, and old out-of-service facility in the middle of nowhere that now houses a tearoom and a museum. Barrie Foulser showed me around the museum, which included a display of incredibly primitive-looking switchboard equipment that had been in use here as recently as the 1980s. There were old-timey bells on the wall; a minuscule switchboard with just a score or so of sockets for connecting lines; clunky old manual typewriters; a heavy black Bakelite telephone. But in April of 1964 the U.S. space program found itself dependent on this equipment.

"Mrs. Lillian O'Donahue was on duty," said Barrie. "NASA's earth station a hundred miles up the coast at Carnarvon was set to track an unmanned Gemini space capsule. Part of the communication line for this ran from Carnarvon to the big tracking station at Woomera, northwest of Adelaide. But lightning knocked out that original line, and communications were channeled through here.

"From 10:30 at night till 3:00 in the morning, Mrs. O'Donahue sat here relaying messages between Carnarvon and Woomera. The connection was so weak she had to repeat all messages in both directions. There were thousands of coded figures that meant nothing to her. The spacecraft made three passes over Australia while she was on duty."

The next day, when the problem had been fixed and the situation explained to her, Mrs. O'Donahue said, "So that's what it was all about. I had no idea." She earned about $6.00 in overtime and a letter of appreciation from her boss.

At Carnarvon, the huge satellite dish that received communications from the spacecraft still stands, though it hasn't been used since 1987. It was on duty all through the U.S. manned space program, and was the first earthly ear to hear Neil Armstrong say, "That's one small step for a man...." It was also the station that broadcast the first satellite TV program in Australia, an exchange between Carnarvon and London called "Down Under Comes Up Live."

Usually the dish is raised and peering toward the horizon, but a cyclone was anticipated in Carnarvon, so technicians had rotated the dish backward till it was facing straight up into the sky, lessening its exposure to wind.

The leading edge of the cyclone and I got to Carnarvon about the same time. At the satellite dish, which is about the size of a small apartment building, the rigging hummed in the gale as the wind whistled through struts and girders, and the huge structure seemed almost to sway, as if it were about to take off. As I stood there, a brown falcon leaped from one of its ledges and soared out over the bush, hanging in the wind like a mobile.

Downtown at the police station in Carnarvon there stands a tall tower with three lights at its top: one red, one yellow, one blue. I found it flashing blue, which meant a cyclone watch was in effect. The cyclone, named Frank—and which the radio immediately began referring to as "Cranky Franky"—was expected to hit the town in the next 24 hours or so.

At noon the light atop the police station tower begins to flash yellow, and the schools close. At the Small Boat Harbour, people are busy securing and lashing down everything that might take off in the wind. At Pelican Point Beach, a reckless windsurfer hurtles to and fro at about 40 miles an hour, spray flying. The sand is blowing so hard it stings my face. As the hours pass, merchants stand outside their places of business, watching the sky and comparing rumors. There's a sense of excitement in town.

Cyclones are the Southern Hemisphere's hurricanes. South of the Equator cyclone winds whirl clockwise, the opposite direction of the north's storms. Tropical cyclones form only over warm oceans—like the waters off northwestern Australia. In circular patterns of storms, they bring torrential rains and winds up to 180 miles an hour. This part of the coast regularly gets hit.

In the night the rains came, but the brunt of the storm missed Carnarvon, causing power losses and damage to the north in Exmouth, where wind speeds exceeded 80 miles an hour. Another nearby town got more than 6 inches of rain in 24 hours.

In the morning we awoke to flooded highways. Here, where coastal flatlands run inland for miles, the highways dip down into small gullies every few miles—gullies that are marked by "FLOOD-WAY" signs but that usually are totally dry. When the rains come, however, the gullies fill with water—which sits. Highways can be covered with several feet of water for days on end.

So I spent a few days longer in Carnarvon than I had intended. Excursions both north and south out of town soon would bring me to places where ugly brown water flowed across the road. It was impossible to tell how deep it was, and while a few big trucks and four–wheel-drive vehicles were making it through, those of us in ordinary automobiles bided our time.

Every morning I would call the highway department—which in Western Australia is called Main Roads; a woman answers the phone, "Main Roads"—and every evening prepare for another night in Carnarvon. Two days after the cyclone, the woman at Main Roads reported that there were still 600 millimeters of water on the road between Carnarvon and Exmouth. It doesn't sound like much in millimeters, but turns out to be about two feet of water.

A couple of days after that, driving the 230 lonely miles from Carnarvon up the coast to Exmouth, I see a highway sign announcing that I am crossing the Tropic of Capricorn. Welcome to the tropics.

Kim McKeown, who had shown me around Margaret River, had a nephew in Exmouth, so I looked him up. Part Crocodile Dundee and part Greg Norman, Neil McLeod is full of fun and enthusiasm. He operates Ningaloo Safari Tours, which totes tourists around the area—especially to nearby Cape Range National Park—and I spent a few days going along.

The park lies along the west coast of North West Cape. It's a narrow but rugged limestone spine of about 125,000 acres, cleft by gullies, and we went up and over it one day in Neil's four-wheel-drive vehicle. "Exmouth was only founded in 1967, as a support town for a joint Australian and U.S. naval communications station," he said, as we traveled. "Most of the Americans are gone now, but many were my good friends when I was growing up." Feral goat trails patterned the hillsides.

Exmouth averages 3,500 hours of sunshine every year, according to Neil, which makes it one of the sunniest places in Australia. It even has its own solar observatory just outside of town.

We stopped at Turquoise Bay for a snorkel, then Neil said, "Let's boil the billy and have some of Mum's orange cake." He uses rainwater for making tea and whirls the teakettle over his head to settle the grounds.

We took a little boat trip up Yardie Creek. Ospreys on their perches stood and stared down at us as we glided by, and black-footed rock wallabies dozed in the sun. One was seated on a ledge, its legs sticking out over the edge like a child's.

Driving home through the dusk, roadside meadows and bush were thick with kangaroos and emus. Like deer in the U.S., they often come to grief crossing highways. Kangaroos especially tend to hop into the paths of oncoming cars, and the unequal battle leaves their furry corpses littering the shoulders.

The next night I accompanied Neil again, this time to Grave-yard Beach, where sea turtles come ashore at night to nest and lay their eggs. Four species of turtles are found here on the northwest coast—green, loggerhead, hawksbill, and flatback. Nesting begins at the end of October. A female, when her time comes, struggles ashore and up the beach to the soft sand dunes. She scrapes away vegetation and forms a body pit with her flippers. Then she excavates a vertical egg chamber with her hind flippers. It takes about 45 minutes before she's satisfied with her nest, and laying the hundred or so eggs takes another 15 minutes. Then she covers the whole thing up and heads back to sea.

We got to the beach just at dark and walked south along it, stumbling in the soft sand and tripping over clumps of grass, straining to see where we were going. With the sun down, a strong sea breeze felt cold. Neil scouted ahead of us and returned, emerging from the darkness: "There are a couple just starting," he said. "While we wait, let's go boil the billy and have a bit of Mum's boiled fruitcake." We stood around the van, sipping tea, eating fruitcake, and getting acquainted—two girls from Sydney, a couple from Queensland, a young Frenchman, a mother and son from Wales.

For several hours that night we watched the turtles. We were careful not to disturb them while they were digging, but once the egg-laying begins they seem oblivious to everything around them. Sprawled behind them with flashlights, we could watch the pile of eggs—like shiny Ping-Pong balls—grow in the pit.

It was sobering to watch the huge, lumbering creatures—they seem so clumsy and helpless on land, and the effort they expend is so intense. It was sobering, too, to know what the likely end will be for most of the hatchlings: When the baby turtles fight their way out of the shell and scurry awkwardly toward the safety of the water, they're easy victims; predators of every sort line up to devour them. Only a fraction of the hatchlings survive more than a few minutes.

One female, finished laying her eggs, headed for the water. We walked alongside her, touching her, taking her picture. It's hard to imagine what dim terror we must have inspired in her, but she was single-minded and plodding and finally disappeared into the creamy surf.

On the way home to Exmouth, we stopped at the Vlaming Head Lighthouse, built in 1912. Inside, Neil's flashlight illuminated unexpected twists and corners as we climbed the curving stairs in the dark, past spooky nooks and crannies. The wind was howling, but the lighthouse stood like the rock it was built on.

Mary Jane Butler, wife of an early keeper here, remembered what it was like to live in so isolated a spot early in the century. She could seldom use the verandas of her house in the evening, she wrote, because "crabs used to come up the beach in their thousands cleaning up everything in their path. The men used to just kick through but I couldn't bear them." She used to make "excellent cakes, custards and omelettes" from turtle eggs.

Having sampled the "excellent cakes" of Neil's mum, I was anxious to meet her and get a copy of her recipes. Neil helped me find her, sorting through donations for the poor at her church in downtown Exmouth. She was tiny and white-haired and full of laughter and energy. She invited us in for tea and apologized because the cakes she served weren't homemade.

"We usually say grace, but we don't for morning tea," she laughed. "We give the Lord a rest."

I asked her how many cakes she had baked over the years for Neil's groups. She said, "There used to be a lovely sister up at the hospital, a midwife. That was in the days when there were babies being born all the time—Exmouth was a young peoples' place then—and I asked her once how many babies she had delivered, and she said, 'Oh, heavens, I've lost count.' I always thought, 'How could you lose count?' But then these cakes came along, and I understand perfectly."

We sipped our tea. "I love making them. I love that three-hours' work at night. Sometimes I doze off while I'm waiting for a cake to bake, and I'll say to Neil, 'This one may be a little dry.' The orange cake is the same I used to make when I was 12. It's foolproof. It really is." I said I'd let her know about that.

She showed me around her church, including a temporary section put up in 1969 and still in use. "On the day of the cyclone I came down to see how things were and sat here worrying, listening to this temporary wall go back and forth. It's all been eaten away by white ants." By herself, she rigged a line from the wall to a firmer foundation on the other side of the room and, with the wall, weathered the storm.

She pressed upon me a couple of chicken wings for my lunch and sent me on my way with a fond, "God bless you." Today when I think of cheerful Australian hospitality, I think of Neil's mum.

Fifty miles of tidal flats dotted with mangrove thickets, islands, and beaches extend north from Exmouth. This region—the Pilbara—also contains rugged inland uplands cut by river valleys and Australia's oldest chunk of crustal rock, the ancient Pilbara block. Beyond it sprawls the Dampier Archipelago—42 islands, 25 of them nature reserves that are havens for native plants and animals. In the late 1600s, when British explorer William Dampier visited here, a hundred or so Aborigines lived on the islands and on the Burrup Peninsula. They have long since gone the way of many of Australia's Aborigines, but they left behind more than 10,000 rock engravings at more than 500 sites.

Karratha is a new town in an old land. It was established in 1971 to serve the booming mining industry. Miaree Pool, a few miles south, is an oasis lined with tall stands of paperbarks, corkwoods, and rivergums where picnickers share the shade and water with birds, fish, and a rare skink found nowhere else. Roebourne, on the other hand, has been a town since the mid-1800s. Its port—Cossack—was once the cosmopolitan center of a thriving pearling industry; it had two Chinese stores and a Chinese bakery, a Japanese store, a Singhalese tailor, and a Turkish bathhouse. Port Hedland, too, was once a pearling port, but now the world's largest ore carriers call in port nearly every day to pick up the Pilbara's most valuable commodity—iron ore. The town's prettiest tidal pool is called Pretty Pool.

For the long, desolate stretch of coast from Port Hedland to Broome—some 360 miles—you have the Indian Ocean on your left and the Great Sandy Desert on your right. There are half-a-dozen places where you can stop for food or shelter—roadhouses and campgrounds—but services are minimal. There's time to anticipate the bright lights and pearl shops of Broome and its famous Cable Beach, nearly 14 miles of exquisite white sand.

The pearls and beaches of Broome are a long way from the sailboats and winding streets of Fremantle, but Australians' enthusiasm for cricket bridges those miles. As I sipped coffee at one roadhouse, I read a newspaper account of a cricket match that began: "Sri Lankan off-spinner Muttiah Muralitharan would again have been no-balled for chucking if he had bowled after tea in the second Test against Australia at the MCG yesterday."

Australia, I was once again reminded, is big and boisterous and enthusiastic, with a lingo and lifestyle all its own.

Sails billowing with breezes from the Indian Ocean, surfcats stand ready to skim the broad Swan River, which links Perth to its port of Fremantle. Capital of Western Australia, Perth is blessed with a Mediterranean climate, a clean river, and extensive beaches, with sailing, fishing, surfing, and swimming at its doorstep. Nearly four out of five of the state's 1.6 million residents live in the sprawling urban area— the remainder are scattered over an expanse nearly four times the size of Texas. Cut off from the rest of Australia by the empty outback and separated from Asia by the Indian Ocean, Perth is one of the world's most isolated cities. In Fremantle (right), a showcase of 19th-century architecture, buildings erected with money made in an 1890s gold rush received a complete facelift when the city hosted the 1987 America's Cup Challenge.

Limbering up with stretches (left), a crew of paddlers prepares for a workout on the Swan River. It takes teamwork to set a long and slender dragon boat (below) into the water; rowers practice in preparation for a regatta held on the Swan on the Chinese New Year. The weather, which lures residents outdoors, and the water, which attracts windsurfers and sailors, make Perth a paradise for the sports-minded.

FOLLOWING PAGES: Trio of galahs, small pink-and-gray cockatoos, enliven the sere landscape and parrot bush scrub of Nambung National Park. Its main attractions are thousands of eerie limestone monoliths up to ten feet in height.

At Beagle Bay Roman Catholic Mission on the Kimberley coast, Aboriginal altar boys gather outside the church before assisting at Mass. In 1989 octogenarian Father Francis preached to his parishioners (above) on the Diamond Jubilee celebrating his 60 years of service at the Aboriginal community. Ornate frames, a local handicraft, use mother-of-pearl from the nearby town of Broome, once the world's main supplier of the iridescent shell.

FOLLOWING PAGES: Terminating abruptly, puzzling tire tracks near Derby demonstrate the demands of driving across the tidal flats of the Kimberley coast. As two vehicles began to bog down, the drivers backed out to avoid being trapped by fast-rising 35-foot tides.

WESTERN WATERS

*Photographed
by David Doubilet*

Arching through nearly 10° of latitude, the western shoulder of Australia encompasses many diverse worlds. The Great Sandy Desert, an arid expanse of endless dunes, backs Eighty Mile Beach, an empty realm virtually unmarked by human footprints. In waters to the southwest lies an Eden—Ningaloo Reef—with a rich array of marine life almost rivaling that of the Great Barrier Reef. Low-lying coastal plains varying in width edge the Indian Ocean. Steep Point, on Shark Bay, is the westernmost limit of the Australian mainland. In 1818-1822 Phillip Parker King made the first true exploration of this coast. The region remains one of the least known parts of Australia.

Rearing up from mangrove-fringed shallows in the Monte Bello Islands, an irritated mud crab waves agile claws with a reach spanning as much as four feet.

Elusive giant, a dugong finds sanctuary and lush grazing in Shark Bay, one of Australia's 11 world heritage areas. Like its manatee cousin, the dugong belongs to the order Sirenia, the only marine mammals subsisting on vegetation.

FOLLOWING PAGES: The richest pearl beds in the world lie in the unpolluted waters off Eighty Mile Beach, south of Broome. Nutrient-rich tides nourish the huge bivalves here.

Accompanied by a flotilla of yellow-striped jacks, manta rays glide through the waters outside Shark Bay, near Australia's westernmost point. The jacks hover near the rays to feed on debris they stir up foraging for plankton.

FOLLOWING PAGES: A jellyfish, a species discovered in 1989, drifts above stromatolites in Shark Bay. These sediment-trapping algae, among earth's first life-forms, grow in clumps.

Alert to the hazards of the world it inhabits, a wallaby comes for a drink in the muddy Ord River, one of the crocodile-infested streams that drain the rugged and remote north coast.

FOLLOWING PAGES: Song and dance of the original Australians—called a corroboree— invoke the ancient Dreamtime in the Aboriginal community of Kalumburu.

THE WILD NORTH

Photographed by Sam Abell

n Australia, it seems, everything is either upside down or backward. The farther north you go, the hotter it gets. The farther south, the colder. People drive on the wrong side of the road. January is midsummer, and July is the dead of winter. Even men's zippers are backward; the part that slides up and down is on the left instead of the right. It took me forever to master getting into and out of a windbreaker I bought.

The topsy-turvy nature of the country is especially noticeable along its upper edge where, even though you are in the far north where it ought to be cool, the Equator is just over the horizon. The wild north has just two seasons—a dry period between April and October, and a hot, humid one the rest of the year, which Aussies call the wet. Humidity during the wet is up around 98 percent for weeks on end, rain falls constantly, and the temperature regularly soars above 100°F.

In Broome, shady verandas look out onto palm-lined streets where tourists wilt in the heat. Skies here are among the world's most dramatic. A taxi driver told me that he and his family sometimes spend hours on the jetty just watching thunderstorms. Broome is in an area called the Kimberley, a virtually empty region of northwestern Australia that covers some 125,000 square miles. Inland is the Great Sandy Desert; the coast is a muddy realm of mangroves and crocodiles.

The waters off Broome sit atop rich oyster beds, and by early in the century the world's button industry, dependent on mother-of-pearl, had made Broome a busy port. As many as 400 pearl luggers worked from its jetty, and hundreds of Japanese divers thronged the streets. When steamers arrived at the jetty and the 30-foot tide went out, the ships sat high and dry. Their passengers disembarked to pose for photos alongside the propellers.

Broome's pearls come from *Pinctada maxima,* largest of the world's 30 species of pearl oysters. Individuals nearly a foot in diameter have been found. Originally, the valuable commodity was the smooth interior of the shell—mother-of-pearl. Broome once provided the raw material for 80 percent of the world's shirt and trouser buttons. In heavy canvas suits and copper helmets, trailing air hoses, divers worked the murky depths off Broome for years. Many were lost to the bends, cyclones, or sharks.

Divers still go down, albeit with more modern equipment. They are still lost. In November 1993 a 27-year-old was killed by a shark while diving in 46 feet of water on one of Broome's pearl farms. His body wasn't found, but some of his clothing was—in the stomach of a tiger shark hooked several days after his disappearance.

Pearls are still big business in Broome, but now they're mostly cultured, grown commercially in pearl farms. The industry began in the mid-1950s; former divers now manage many of the farms.

I visited the Willie Creek Pearl Farm with a group of tourists. The manager took us down to the tidal flats, where seeded oysters are loaded into metal racks and dangled in the water; the strong tides here wash back and forth across them four times a day, feeding them. An irritant—oddly, a piece of mussel shell from Mississippi—has been carefully introduced into the animal, around which a pearl will grow. We watched as our guide gingerly opened an oyster and removed the pearl inside. "Oysters can grow maybe three pearls," he said. "Then they're...retired."

Offshore, Indonesian fishing boats sometimes get in trouble, entering restricted waters in quest of sea cucumber—or bêche-de-mer, which is popular for making soup in China—as well as trochus shell—used in making jewelry—and clams. When officials confiscate foreign boats, they often store them in Willie Creek, not far from the pearl farm. Eight, with a total crew of about 70, were being held there. They had been stopped at Hibernia Reef, 500 nautical miles north of Broome. More than 125 Indonesian boats had been confiscated in the last three months of 1994.

My next stop was Derby, a hot little town full of red dust and boab trees. Its main street has a long greenway planted with the odd-shaped things. Boabs grow only in the Kimberley and adjacent parts of the Northern Territory. They're in keeping with Australia's upside-down nature. They look like they're growing with their roots in the air. According to legend, one hollow giant a few miles out of town was once used as a prison by police; Aborigines charged with crimes and awaiting trial were held in its 46-foot girth. The tree may be more than a thousand years old.

In 1883 two sheep stations near Derby lost their entire wool harvest in a tsunami that followed the eruption of Krakatoa, 1,450 miles away in Indonesia. Even under normal conditions, tides here can reach 35 feet, making them the highest in the southern hemisphere. They cause quite a stir north of Derby as they sweep among the bays and islands of the Buccaneer Archipelago. I got a little plane to take me for a look.

We flew over scores of islets—there are several hundred—and past Point Torment, where early explorers were plagued by sand flies and mosquitoes. At Pasco Island, the rushing tide was turbulent and white. Pearl boats were anchored nearby. Moored lines held dangling racks of oysters; they looked like stitching on the surface of the ocean. A huge cargo ship was anchored at the wharf of Cockatoo Island loading iron ore. Bungalows of a failed resort dotted one end of the island, the swimming pool still an inviting blue.

Nearby, two bays stretched out beside each other, each with an entrance just a few feet wide; coming and going, the tide rushes through these tiny openings. During an incoming tide, the ocean rises faster than water can enter; it stacks up and rushes through in a river of white water. The same thing happens when the tide goes out—the bays try to empty themselves faster than the water can escape. Locals call these unusual features "a horizontal waterfall." They reminded me of the rushing white-water rapids of the American West.

Western Australia's nearly inaccessible northern edge, above the Great Sandy Desert and along the Timor Sea, is crinkled with ranges of sandstone and limestone formations. Near the coast are tropical woodlands, vine thickets, paperbark swamps, riverine forests of coolibahs and cadjeputs, and the ever-present mangroves. Communities of 12 species of mangroves form broad, thick forests up to 50 feet tall. Their fallen leaves contribute to a food chain for marine animals. Every square yard of tropical mangrove forest yields about two pounds of organic material every year.

Between Broome and Wyndham, which anchors the Kimberley's eastern edge, the coast is virtually inaccessible except by boat or plane. This is the territory of *Crocodylus porosus*—the fearsome saltwater crocodile, the grinning reptile whose knobby eyebrows and nostrils break the surface of muddy streams all across the tropical top of Australia. Brown rivers empty into the sea, and yachts sometimes anchor in them. Aboard one that tied up several years ago in the Prince Regent River was a young woman from Virginia named Ginger Meadows. Unaccountably unaware of the threat from salties in the area, Ginger and a companion went for a swim. Warned at last of the presence of the animals, the women climbed onto a ledge. As a crocodile approached, Ginger made a break for dry ground. She never got there.

A clipping at the Wyndham historical society said, "Wyndham is perversely proud of being the hottest town in Australia." The town has the country's highest average temperature and would hold the record for the longest string of days above a hundred degrees but for a sudden change in the wind; it shifted six hours too soon and the record stayed in nearby Halls Creek.

Certainly Wyndham was the hottest place I've ever been. One day, when I stopped by my motel for a refreshing shower in mid-afternoon, the water that came from the *cold* tap was nearly too hot to stand under. The town's water supply comes from up in the hills through a metal pipe and gets heated by the sun all day.

Five rivers—the Pentecost, Ord, Forrest, King, and Durack—converge at Wyndham and empty into the Timor Sea. From Five

Rivers Lookout they can be seen, running across miles of tidal mudflats, winding slowly toward the coast. One afternoon I watched thunderstorms on all four horizons flicker and boom and drop pale curtains of rain. Nothing came to cool Wyndham.

Mike Osborn, then manager of the Wyndham croc farm, and I got a little plane and flew over the coast. Tracks of a large turtle on a beach looked like the treads of an armored vehicle. The Timor Sea on our right was shallow and brown, and the rough and desolate coast looked—and was—uninhabited. Tidal flats had fingers of green vegetation where streams crossed them. Above the Ord River, Mike said, "The tidal reaches of the Ord have more salties per kilometer than any other river system in the Kimberley." I tried to spot them from the plane but couldn't.

We flew up the Berkeley River to red sandstone gorges 300 feet high and the King George River to its falls, dry now—a pretty spot where yachtsmen like to anchor; the water is deep enough that they can tie up practically under the torrent. On we flew, to the Drysdale River, then above an island that was the site of a World War II base, and over the site of an old mission where there's a grave of an American serviceman taken by a crocodile.

Darwin, tucked away near the very top of the continent, has had a tough time keeping its roof on over the years. In 1897 and again in 1937 cyclones leveled what was then a frontier town. A storm of another sort hit in 1942: Darwin was bombed 64 times by the Japanese that year, The first two raids, only hours apart, killed 243 people, including the postmaster. Because of the number of ships sunk here, Darwin's harbor is strewn with official war graves.

On Christmas Day of 1974 another cyclone—Tracy—flattened the city: 160-mile-an-hour winds destroyed more than 9,000 homes in a 4-hour period. More than 60 people were killed in what is still Australia's worst natural disaster.

So Darwin, beneath its blazing sun and tropical skies, keeps rebuilding itself, this time as a wide-avenued city with banyan and mango trees lining its streets. Its harbor was discovered in 1839 by a party exploring off the H.M.S. *Beagle* and named for the naturalist who had sailed aboard the ship a few years earlier. The town that arose was the first permanent settlement in the north.

During the war the Northern Territory from Darwin to the little town of Alice Springs, 900 miles south, became the base for tens of thousands of troops. For the first time, a road was built between Darwin and the railhead at Alice Springs, deep in the country's arid heart. It fell far short of the demands of wartime: In a rainy five-week period in 1941 and 1942, up to a hundred vehicles at a time bogged down. American engineers and equipment came to help rebuild it. To care for the war wounded, some 35 hospitals and convalescent camps were spread across the Northern Territory; to launch aircraft against Japan, by July 1942 there were more than 60 airfields and strips in the region around Darwin. You can see their remnants today, as you drive south; small roadside signs identify gravel strips just off the road.

One of Australia's most famous national parks hugs the coastline east of Darwin. Kakadu derived its name from a local Aboriginal language—Gagudju. At nearly 5 million acres, Kakadu is Australia's largest park, sprawling 75 miles from east to west and 130 miles from north to south. Gagudju Aborigines share in its management. Kakadu is largely floodplains backed by the cliffs of the Arnhem Land Escarpment, which runs for about 300 miles through the Northern Territory. The park encompasses wetlands, billabongs, streams, gorges, grasslands, and eucalyptus forests, as well as the wildlife that goes with them. Aborigines have lived in this area for more than 40,000 years; the sandstone walls, rock faces, and caves are richly daubed with their artwork. Some 5,000 art sites have been documented in the park, and as many more exist.

Rafferty Fynn, tall, dark, and handsome—a young Peter O'Toole look-alike—was my guide into Kakadu and nearby Litchfield National Park. Four of us—a plastic surgeon from Los Angeles; a Japanese college student and her aunt, who spoke only one bit of English: "Sank you"; and myself—signed on with Rafferty for a four-day tour. It was not yet the wet season, but it was getting close, and the heat and humidity were ferocious. From the rain that fell that first day, you might have thought it was midwet. It came down in fierce buckets. The Land Cruiser's windshield wipers made not a dent in the torrent.

Rafferty had eyes like a wedge-tailed eagle and stopped the Land Cruiser with a lurch that first day. "Wait here," he said, and set off into the roadside forest. Somehow he had spotted a frilled lizard the color of bark clinging to a tree 30 yards away. He returned to us with the startled creature clinging to his arm, its beautifully mottled neck ruff opened wide, like an umbrella, its fearsome mouth gaping wide, hissing. Released, it got up onto its hind legs and scurried furiously back into the forest.

Litchfield National Park has some famous waterfalls—especially Florence and Wangi—that drop spectacularly into pools where we, along with other tourists, cooled off. We saw dingoes, lots of kites, and a blue-winged kookaburra, whose voice, according to my bird book, is "extended maniac laughter."

We spent a couple of nights at Katherine, a town named for its nearby river. In 1862 explorer John McDouall Stuart named the river for a daughter of one of his benefactors. We visited a nearby military cemetery, where locals killed in World War II were buried. Several graves were marked with only a single name: Sheila, Magi, Henry—Aborigines with no last names. The Darwin postmaster and his family were also buried here.

One day we stopped by Manyallaluk—"the Dreaming Place"— a 1,160 square-mile Aboriginal community. It is a traditional home of the Jawoyn Aboriginal people, and its name honors a frog-dreaming site just to the east of the settlement.

Darryl Miller and Ricky Nelson, two young men barely out of their teens, walked us through the bush, pointing out plants used as either food or medicine by their Aboriginal ancestors. Darryl had gone to high school in Darwin.

"Did you like Darwin?" I asked him.

"A little bit," he said. "Too many cars, eh?"

They later demonstrated bark painting and spear throwing and making a fire by rubbing sticks together, while women of the community, sitting cross-legged on the ground and laughing among themselves, wove handsome and sturdy baskets.

Through the huge landscape we hurtled, kicking up clouds of dust, Handel's "The Arrival of the Queen of Sheba" playing on Rafferty's tape deck. The Land Cruiser's air-conditioning kept the awful heat at bay, but we all wilted badly after excursions on foot. In afternoons, the vehicle would grow very quiet, as some of us indulged in after-lunch naps.

We stopped to see fields full of termite mounds, some of them nine feet tall, hatchet-blade bulwarks standing in rows, all oriented north to south. "They're lined up like that so the full force of the afternoon sun doesn't hit them," said Rafferty. "It's how the termites control the temperature inside their nests." At a colony of green tree ants, Rafferty collected a few and showed us how to quickly crunch them between our teeth, before they bit us, and chew their lemony essence. He passed some around. "Sank you," said the aunt.

On our way back to Darwin, at Shady Camp Reserve, we went for a couple of boat rides on the Mary River and on a freshwater billabong nearby with Michael Egan, the only person I ever expect to meet from the town of Humpty Doo. Near the billabong's banks, long-legged jacanas strolled on the lily pads, and cormorants watched us from the tops of bare trees.

"I think this will be Australia's next national park," said Michael, as we drifted along. "Shady Camp was named by John McDouall Stuart, who called it 'intensely forested.' Now you can see what it's become." Much of the countryside nearby looked like scrubby rangeland. "Settlers brought in water buffalo, which got away and began to reproduce in the wild. A region that throughout history had never felt a cloven hoof, within a hundred years had 300,000 water buffalo on it. There were up to 300 of the animals per square kilometer. They devegetated the entire area. Disease got rid of them, but in an unusual way. The U.S. wouldn't import Australian beef as long as brucellosis and tuberculosis were at large in populations of feral cattle, so the government began eradicating the herds. The area's forests are coming back nicely."

Back at the landing, we all loaded into our vehicles and drove five minutes to another boat at another landing, this one on a saltwater, tidal section of the Mary River. The tide was out, and the river's black mud banks sloped back for hundreds of yards. The sun was about to set, and the banks were just coming to life: a crocodile here, a crocodile there, then a couple more. Our eyes became adept at picking them out, mud-colored creatures lazing in black muck. A pair of eyebrows and nostrils trailed a V-shaped wake across the still water. Then another, and another. Then dozens, then scores of crocodiles were all around us in the evening. "Everybody keep your elbows in the boat," said Michael.

"There are more saltwater crocodiles per kilometer in the Mary than in any other river system on earth. It gives you a good idea of the richness of the food chain here." Huge crocs lay immobile at the edge of the water until we got too close; then with a tremendous explosion of power and splashing they lunged into the water. It was eerie to think of the dozens of them that must be right under our boat. "Big crocs eat little crocs, so they've learned to fear each other," said Michael. "They think our boat is a huge crocodile. They'll sit very still until they can't stand it any longer, then they'll flee."

Schools of tiny mullet skittered along the surface of the river, literally flying in their panicky haste. "When you're at the bottom of the food chain, you tend to be a little jumpy," said Michael.

Abutting Kakadu on the east is 37,000-square-mile Arnhem Land, one of the largest of many hundreds of parcels of Aboriginal land in Australia. Matthew Flinders named the region for the *Arnhem*, the ship of an early Dutch explorer. About a fourth of the Northern Territory's population are Aborigines, who own more than 40 percent of the territory.

Australia's first inhabitants came to the island continent about 60,000 years ago, probably in small groups and probably from Southeast Asia. They spread out to cover every part of the continent. When Europeans arrived, the Aborigines likely numbered about 900,000. There were perhaps 700 different tribes, each living in a particular homeland and speaking its own language or dialect. They lived by hunting and gathering, moving throughout their territory, occasionally getting together with other groups for trading and religious ceremonies.

Complex kinship systems governed marriage eligibility, responsibilities, and taboo relationships, and religious beliefs were based on the Dreamtime, a period when mythic spirits shaped the land, bringing into being human, animal, and plant life. The spirits were eternal, and some transformed themselves into certain prominent and sacred landforms.

Both oral and visual arts were highly developed throughout the country, with many communities producing fine bark and cave paintings, rock engravings, and sculptured posts and figures. The Aborigines of Arnhem Land produced elaborate song cycles that made use of complex symbolic allusion and imagery.

In 1992, in a famous and far-reaching court case, Australia's Aborigines won the right to reclaim their traditional lands. Until then, since the time of Captain Cook, the doctrine of *terra nullius* had prevailed—that Australia was no-man's-land, unoccupied when Cook landed. Only ancestral land that belongs to the government can be claimed; in Australia that now amounts to about 5 percent of the country.

Brian Rooke and his wife Phyllis Williams own and operate Umorrduk Safaris, offering trips into Arnhem Land. Brian is descended from Bass Strait Islands Aborigines, and Phyllis's family, of the Gummulkbun Aboriginal clan, has lived in Arnhem Land for countless generations. Her clan claimed and got possession of the Mudjeegarrdart, a tract of some 250,000 acres in western Arnhem Land. I flew with them from Darwin to their camp at Umorrduk. We traveled for about an hour across miles of muddy coastline, with brown rivers and streams meandering across flat mud plains before emptying themselves into the ocean.

The landing strip was a bumpy ribbon of grass in the middle of the bush; outside the plane the suffocating heat settled upon us like a wet blanket. In a four-wheel drive—with wallabies bounding across the track in front of us—we made our way to Umalgee billabong, where thousands of birds were gathered: magpie geese, egrets, ibises, tall and majestic jabirus, which are Australia's only storks. The trees were full of corellas making a fierce noise.

We boiled the billy for tea and sat on camp stools in the shade. Dingoes in the bush watched us with lazy, contemptuous indifference; flocks of geese arriving at the billabong floated over us, the air rushing audibly through their wings.

After lunch we drove to an enormous rock outcrop named Mabaloodoo. Like a magic castle, Mabaloodoo rises above its surroundings and is riddled with archways, caves, ledges, and natural stairways. And everywhere is ancient rock art: on walls, ceilings, under overhangs.

There were paintings of animals and men and mythical beings. Some overlapped; some were faint with age, others looked like they had been painted yesterday. One whole wall was painted with food sources—kangaroos and snakes, fish and birds.

To the east of Arnhem Land lies the enormous indentation of the Gulf of Carpentaria—a shallow inlet of the Arafura Sea. Shaped like a horseshoe, it extends about 400 miles from east to west and nearly 500 miles from north to south. From its warm waters, fishermen pluck prawns and barramundi—a large and delicious fish found in Aboriginal paintings dating back as far as 10,000 years. Barramundi can grow to be huge: Some reach 5 feet in length and weigh up to 90 pounds.

They spawn in the warm waters of the mouths of rivers between October and February. The tiny new fish, preyed upon by just about everything, hide among coastal mangroves and in swamps around tidal estuaries, then make their way upstream after the wet-season floods subside. They spend several years in deep pools and freshwater reaches of larger rivers. When they are about one and a half feet long and three to four years old, they move back downstream to saltwater to breed. Almost all the fish of this size are males, and they remain so until they're between six and eight years old, when they change to females.

As if running a gauntlet of predators weren't dangerous enough, barramundi are the prime targets of fishermen all around the gulf. The demand for barramundi throughout Australia is great. Despite its small size, Karumba today exports some two million Australian dollars worth of barramundi every year.

The barramundi population in Australia is dwindling, and a group of people in Karumba, at the head of the gulf, is trying to do something to help them.

Karumba was another of those hot little towns, with broad dusty streets bumping into the sluggish Norman River. A wide concrete ramp running down into the river survives from the days when Karumba was an important base for flying boats—amphibious aircraft that flew a route between Sydney and England. I had some fish and chips in the town's café—barramundi, of course—then went to meet Neil Tulau, a member of the Gulf Barra Restocking Association.

Down by the river, in a dim, garage-like building, he showed me a tall tank full of water and its denizens. At a porthole in the side of the tank, grim visages appeared: the thin, pointed faces of adult barramundi. Their jaws worked as they breathed. Something about the light made their eyes shine like a deer's in auto headlights. They looked spooky and otherworldly.

"These are local fish from our river here," said Neil. "The biggest female weighs about 35 pounds. We inject hormones into them to get them started breeding, and we'll get between 10 and 15 million eggs at a time from this big female." Up a ladder to the top of the tank he went, carrying a bucket of pilchards. "Sometimes we add vitamins to the pilchards," he said, dropping the fish one by one into the tank. You could hear the mighty whack of powerful jaws as the barramundi ate. Outside were two big man-made ponds, dry now. "We fill the ponds with seawater and allow plankton to bloom. When the barramundi are about an eighth of an inch long, we release them into the ponds. After a couple of days they begin feeding on the plankton. At three weeks they become predators, so they must be released or they'd start eating each other. We can't afford to buy food for them."

The effort to build up the barramundi population is funded largely by fishermen and their organizations, with some help from the Queensland and local governments.

"We're trying to eliminate the most dangerous period in a young barra's life," said Neil, "when they're first born and are prey to everything and spend their time traveling between salt-water and fresh. We release them upstream and eliminate that gauntlet. It takes them about three years to grow to catchable size. When I first came to Karumba 20 years ago, you could go out and throw a line in the water and catch a barra. Now you can't." Figures indicate that about 20 to 30 percent of the hatched fish survive in the wild, as opposed to perhaps less than 1 percent of those born naturally, so the effort seems to be paying off.

The next day I asked Neil to show me a nearby landmark that had long held my imagination. In 1860 an expedition set off from Melbourne to cross the Australian continent from south to north. The Burke and Wills expedition was led by an immigrant Irish policeman—Robert O'Hara Burke—and hoped to find a transcontinental route through the mysterious interior of Australia. William John Wills, later Burke's partner, was appointed surveyor. With the help of camels, suffering terrible hardships, leaving caches of supplies and men at various points, Burke and Wills inched across Australia. It took them six months to go the 1,650 miles to the Gulf of Carpentaria. Their last campsite— Camp 119— was a few miles south of Karumba.

From there, on Sunday, February 10, carrying three days' rations, Burke and Wills set out on a final dash to the gulf, leaving the remaining two men and the camels behind. That night they camped on boggy ground, and the water in a channel was brackish with an eight-inch tide. They had crossed the continent. They weren't able to reach the actual shoreline for the swamps and the mangroves, and didn't get to see the ocean. On the return, heartbreakingly, they arrived at a supply depot at Cooper Creek just hours after the party there had given up on them and headed home. Burke and Wills both died at the creek within months, possibly of a vitamin deficiency.

Today Camp 119 is lonely and desolate, surrounded by miles of bush. A couple of memorials have been erected, including, oddly, a lamppost from Brisbane with a neat fence around it, and a plaque from the Royal Geographical Society of Australasia honoring "the first successful crossing south to north of the Australian continent...." Burke and Wills had been here during the wet, when their animals were forever getting bogged, but it was dry as dust during my visit. The landscape was perfectly featureless. Red-tailed black cockatoos shrieked at us from the treetops.

As for my trip around the continent, there remained only the tip of Cape York. It's as far north as you can go on the Australian mainland, slightly more than ten degrees south of the Equator.

As elsewhere in Australia, the Aboriginal population of Cape York Peninsula was decimated by its contact with Europeans. But around the turn of the century, the remains of several seminomadic family tribes who lived in the last 125 miles of the peninsula came together and settled at the mouth of a creek. They developed into an independent and self-supporting community—Injinoo—which even today prefers to go its own way. Among other initiatives, the Injinoo operate the Pajinka Wilderness Lodge at the tip of the cape.

Hot there? I was sitting one day beneath an open-air ceiling fan, a cold drink in one hand and another fan in the other, melting into my chair, when one of the staff strolled by, whistling and jolly. He saw me there. "She's a bit tropical today, eh?"

Pajinka is a birder's paradise. Their bird list has 213 birds on it, out of Australia's 750 or so total species. And in the early mornings the sounds in the forest are of birds and nothing else: You try to listen to the call of a certain bird but the calls of a dozen others, overlapping, drown it out.

I found at Pajinka the most enthusiastic birder I'd ever met—Rob Berry, from Melbourne. His wife, Gail, is cheerfully tolerant of his obsession, and the two of them had come to Pajinka just for the birding. Rob has adapted a couple of computer programs to his hobby and can produce a printout of, for instance, all the birds he has not yet seen in the dry scrub country of New South Wales, or all the birds of a particular family he has or has not seen. And so on. He had recorded about 400 of Australia's birds and had a handful he wanted to find at Pajinka.

He and the guide-naturalist went over his bird list. Of a particular robin, Rob said, "I've heard them everywhere, but can't spot them." He was especially hopeful of seeing a buff-breasted paradise-kingfisher.

I tagged along early one morning as the threesome tiptoed slowly through the woods, looking for birds. "Bird calls are 80 percent of birding here," said the guide. Rob had a serious-looking pair of binoculars around his neck, and a heavy-duty leather holster held his field guide, a notebook, and pens. Whenever he spotted an unfamiliar bird he would whip out his bird book, like a gunslinger. "Pretty quick on the draw, isn't he?" said Gail. There was the sound of wings in the treetops overhead, and rustling in the brush—a mound builder. The call of a frilled monarch—a beautiful pied flycatcher with a white collar—brought everybody to a halt. I glimpsed it briefly. Rob called my attention to a small bird with a blue cap. "Lovely fairy wren," he said.

"Beautiful," I murmured.

"No, that's its name: 'lovely fairy wren.'"

A little trail, marked with white blazes and small cairns, runs from the lodge to the tip of Cape York, the very shoreline where the continent ends. I walked out there one day and sat on the boulders, watching freighters in the distance plowing slowly eastward. The tide rushing between the tip of the mainland and two small islands confused and roiled the waters. Terns shrieked overhead. A metal signpost, its feet in the surf, held a notice: "YOU ARE STANDING AT THE NORTHERNMOST POINT OF THE AUSTRALIAN CONTINENT."

I had been all the way around Australia, nearly back to Cooktown where I had begun. In *The Coast Dwellers,* author Philip Drew calls Australia's coast "the veranda of the continent." One in four Australians now lives within a 15-minute drive of the beach, he points out, which is a great natural veranda to match the man-made ones that provide cool shade to so many Australian homes. I sat on the boulders, Australia's veranda, with the terns and the freighters and the tide.

Turning their backs on the great empty interior of their country and looking instead seaward makes Australians what they have become: worldly and open, welcoming and hospitable, but at the same time grateful for the security and shelter a veranda offers.

Ropes and ties barely contain a saltwater crocodile bound for a park in Perth.
This Wyndham giant terrorized a resident's yard until Mike Osborn, here checking the
rigging, captured him. Mike and his wife, Anne (opposite), managed a croc farm in
Wyndham from 1994 to 1996. At feeding time, a plucked chicken—or "chook," in Aussie
vernacular—disappears down a croc's gullet amid roiling water. Hunters nearly
exterminated northern Australia's two species of crocs—saltwater and freshwater—until
imposed bans sparked the reptiles' recovery. Only "salties" are feared as man-eaters.

PRECEDING PAGES: Frail green traceries rim tidal waters of the Kimberley.
High tides and monsoons here create miles of uninhabitable mudflats along the lonely coast.

F ingers of nature and the hands of man mark the territory of the far north. Filigrees define
a drainage of the Keep River (opposite). Twelve species of mangroves line these northern
shores. Ancient Aborigines left their signs on a sandstone cliff near Wyndham.
Long gouges resulted from millennia of spear and tool sharpening. Stencil-like handprints
were made by spatter painting—spraying a mouthful of pigment over the artist's hand.

"The most heroic and the most hopeless enterprise in British empire history," a naval officer once called Victoria Settlement on the shores of Port Essington. Established in 1838 to forestall Dutch and French expansion in the area, this settlement in one of the most inhospitable spots on the continent never had a chance. Its settlers bravely built thatched-roof cottages, a government house, and planted vegetable gardens. The settlers and local Aborigines worked and lived in harmony, but the isolation, the climate, and such ailments as malaria, dysentery, and influenza soon took their toll. At times, half the garrison was hospitalized. English architecture resulted in low-slung, airless quarters, whose stone chimneys still rise above incongruous fireplaces. Seven Spirit Bay Resort, which leases the land from its Aboriginal owners, today conducts tours of the site; in an old engraving (lower) it bustles with activity.

R*ed-winged parrot perches on bending stalks to munch spear grass seed in open*

country near Nhulunbuy in Arnhem Land, a 37,000-square-mile Aboriginal homeland.

Jim Jim Falls hides its beauty, flowing only during the wet, when flooded roads prevent visitors from reaching the remote site; during the dry season, when tourists arrive, the falls dry up. At 590 feet, it is the highest waterfall in Kakadu National Park, Australia's largest reserve. Kakadu, one of the country's most popular parks, encompasses nearly the entire drainage system of the South Alligator River; the East Alligator floodplain fronts the distant Arnhem Land Escarpment (above).

Members of the oldest surviving culture in the world, Aborigines have called the Gulf of Carpentaria region home for perhaps 60,000 years. In a cooling sprinkle, Nalkuma Burarrwanga (opposite) fishes for giant trevally off Port Bradshaw. The galpu, or woomera, in his hand—an ancient implement—provides extra speed and force when used to hurl a spear. Sam Colin (above) inspects a midden of shells and ancestral remains in coastal country south of the Mitchell River, part of a 2,000-square-mile tract now owned and managed by local Aborigines. The early European policy of terra nullius enforced a legal presumption for centuries that Australia was officially unoccupied. The Australian High Court overturned that policy in 1992, clearing the way for all Australia's Aborigines to lay claim to their traditional homelands.

W*here the river meets the sea, the tannin-tinted waters of the Jardine contrast dramatically with the pale green of the Gulf of Carpentaria (opposite). Here, near the very tip of Cape York Peninsula, New Guinea lies just a hundred miles over the horizon. Few places on earth are less hospitable to mankind. Frank Jardine, whose name attaches to the river, wrote of "the mosquitoes and the bogs and scrubs of this villainous country," but beauty lies all around, as in the pattern of shells on an isolated beach near Kowanyama.*

FOLLOWING PAGES: Evening falls on the Aurukun wetlands as magpie geese soar over sunlit pandanus trees. Beneath them the mounds of termites, vital to the region as recyclers of dead wood and grass, rise like tombstones, and water lilies blanket a peaceful lagoon.